This Book
Belongs to
        Minnie Mann
33 Cherry Hill Crescent
        Dundonald

HOW THE GOSPEL CAME TO BRITAIN

BRIAN WILLIAMS

"The isles shall wait for His law"
—*Isaiah 42: 4*

BRIAN WILLIAMS EVANGELISTIC ASSOCIATION LTD.
BIRMINGHAM, ENGLAND

BOOKS BY THE SAME AUTHOR

Why I Pray for the Sick
Healing from Christ
Jesus Is Coming Very Soon
The Divine Key to Financial Prosperity
The Gospel with Evidence
The Healing Word
The Holy Communion
Water Baptism
Judgment on Britain
Britain in Prophecy
Britain's Royal Throne
How the Gospel Came to Britain
Man in Space!

CONTENTS

ACKNOWLEDGMENTS

The author wishes to acknowledge the following sources of illustrations appearing in this book: Miss G. M. Hodges for the photograph facing page 4, Norman Heal for the photographs facing pages 44, 52 and 60, Central Press Photos Ltd. for the photograph facing page 36, and Keystone Press Agency Ltd. for that facing page 92. The colour photographs were taken by the author. The map facing page 37 appears in *The Rebellion of Boudicca* by D. R. Dudley and Graham Webster and is reproduced with acknowledgment to the publishers, Routledge & Kegan Paul. The author wishes to express his gratitude to Miss Helene W. van Woelderen and Mr. W. A. Koppejan who put *Zebulon Hove* at his disposal where much of the book was written, to Miss Janet M. Jones who provided the Index, and to his secretary Miss Jean A. Fitzpatrick, who assisted in every stage of the preparation of this book.

ILLUSTRATIONS

Made and printed in Great Britain by
Reliance Printing Works, Halesowen

CHAPTER ONE

WHAT HAPPENED TO THE TWELVE APOSTLES?

IN the grounds of Glastonbury Abbey in the South-western county of Somerset there stands a large wooden cross erected in the earth. Unlike the centuries-old ruins which stand close by, the oak cross is a new one, placed there in 1955, and a notice in front of it reads:

THE CROSS
THE SYMBOL OF OUR FAITH
THE GIFT OF
QUEEN ELIZABETH II
MARKS A CHRISTIAN
SANCTUARY SO ANCIENT
THAT ONLY LEGEND
CAN RECORD ITS ORIGIN

Today, a bustling market town of some 6,000 inhabitants, and dominated by the famous Tor, Glastonbury attracts thousands of visitors from around the world. On the last Saturday of June each year a pilgrimage is held when all members of the Church of England, those in communion with her, and all "separated brethren", are invited to share in the act of penitence and devotion.

It is impossible not to be touched by the sanctity of the place There is a feeling of treading on holy ground, and here in the quiet and peacefulness of the Abbey ruins one stands upon "the holyest earthe in England".

For on this spot, without a doubt, was established the earliest Christian foundation in these Isles. Here was erected the first Christian place of worship. Here saints were buried, and to this place have come pilgrims from all over the world. Here in former

7

days stood a great Abbey Church renowned for its sanctity and learning. Before that there existed for several centuries the " ealde chyrche " said to have been built by Christ Himself. And now today as one surveys the Abbey ruins, strangely beautiful and impressive amidst the lawns and trees, the present mingles with the past, tradition and history become inextricably woven together and one is left wondering about all the wonderful associations that this place has for us.

Even the name Glastonbury—the writer pronounces it *Glassenbury* without the ' t '—may have a spiritual connotation. While there is much conjecture as to its derivation and it may mean simply ' Green-hill-borough ', a student of etymology says that the name written in Hebrew form would denote a *fountain* or *spring*—GLA, or *secret*—ST—*bowl* or *reservoir*. An ancient name for Glastonbury was **Ynis Witryn**, again denoting a *fountain* or *spring* in a particular place *between two hills*, while the name Somerset similarly transliterated into Hebrew would mean *the heavens established upon earth.*

As we shall see, Glastonbury was once part of an island known as the Isle of Avilion, *Isle of Spirits,* or Isle of Avalon, *Isle of Apples.* Even the name Avalon takes on new significance in the light of its Hebrew interpretation which is *Beloved Dwelling.* Again, the Tor reminds us of the Hebrew *Torah* or *Law,* while Chalice, associated with Glastonbury's Chalice Well, denotes a Hebrew measure. Then Camelot, only 12 miles from Glastonbury and with its Arthurian connections, could mean *Assembly of God.*

Whether these derivations (by Mrs. R. E. Hovey in *The Messenger of Chalice Well,* No. 7, 3rd Quarter, 1968) are legitimate we cannot say, but they are remarkably significant, for in Glastonbury's remote past are enshrined the origins of the Christian faith in Britain.

But all legend has a foundation in fact, and the purpose of this book is to attempt to present the Glastonbury tradition in the light of the Bible, to sift truth from error wherever possible, and, above all, to stir an interest in the early history of our nation with which all too few are familiar but which should be known by every inhabitant of these Isles. Man has landed upon the moon; huge strides are being made in science and technology and in every field of human endeavour. But we cannot, without a true knowledge of the past and an intelligent understanding of our history, discern God's purpose for us at this hour, and that is our nation's greatest need, for, " Where there is no vision, the people perish."[1]

We said that here at Glastonbury was established the earliest Christian foundation in these Isles. This takes us right back to the foundations of the Christian faith. When did the gospel first come to Britain? Who were the missionaries who were entrusted with the good news, and who were the people in whose hearts it first summoned a response?

The Bible is strangely silent concerning what happened to the Twelve Apostles. The only inspired history of the early Church is given in the Acts of the Apostles, yet remarkably most of the Twelve Apostles are not even mentioned. Peter disappears from the story very early—we do not hear of him again after Acts 15— and most of the book is about the Apostle Paul who was not even listed amongst the original twelve! If the other Apostles are not mentioned we reasonably infer that they were absent from Palestine. So, where were they?

Notice what the Bible tells us about their commission. " And when He had called unto Him His twelve disciples, He gave them power against unclean spirits, to cast them out, and to heal all manner of sickness and all manner of disease. Now the names of the twelve apostles are these; the first, Simon, who is called PETER, and ANDREW his brother; JAMES the son of Zebedee, and JOHN his brother; PHILIP, and BARTHOLOMEW; THOMAS, and MATTHEW the publican; JAMES the son of Alphæus, and LEBBÆUS, whose surname was Thaddæus; SIMON the Canaanite, and JUDAS ISCARIOT, who also betrayed Him. These twelve Jesus sent forth, and commanded them, saying, *Go not into the way of the Gentiles,* and into any city of the Samaritans enter ye not: but go rather to the LOST SHEEP OF THE HOUSE OF ISRAEL. And as ye go, preach, saying, The kingdom of heaven is at hand ".[2]

Now we are usually told that Jesus sent His Apostles to preach to the Jews, and that when the Jews rejected their message they then went to the Gentiles, but that is not what the Bible says! Notice, Jesus commissioned the Twelve to go to the lost sheep of the house of Israel. *He specifically forbade any venture to the Gentiles.* Jesus Himself said, " I am not sent but unto the lost sheep of the house of Israel ".[3]

The lost sheep of the house of Israel were the descendants of the ten tribes which had been taken captive into Assyria[4] between 735-670 B.C. These tribes never returned to Palestine.[5] In the purposes of God they were to lose their identity,[6] become settled in a new home,[7] become a redeemed Christian people,[8] and ultimately become His witnesses,[9] the instrument by which the gospel should be preached throughout the earth.

So, since the Apostles were sent to the lost sheep of the house of Israel but are scarcely mentioned in the Acts of the Apostles, they must have been fulfilling their commission elsewhere. Therefore if we can discover where the Apostles went, *we shall know where God's Israel people were located at that time.*

We do know from the Bible that they were not in Palestine. James addresses his epistle " to the twelve tribes which are *scattered abroad* ".[10] Peter addresses his letter " to the *strangers* scattered throughout Pontus, Galatia, Cappadocia, Asia, and Bithynia ".[11] The word ' strangers ' means *God's elect people in exile.* Evidently some, though not all, of the tribes of Israel were domiciled in those places, part of what we should now call Asia Minor.

Now the Book of Acts—the *inspired* history of the New Testament Church—was written by the physician Luke who also wrote the Gospel which bears his name. Notice how he commences his account. " The former treatise have I made, O Theophilus, of all that Jesus began both to do and teach, until the day in which He was taken up, after that He through the Holy Ghost had given commandments unto THE APOSTLES WHOM HE HAD CHOSEN: to whom also He shewed Himself alive after His passion by many infallible proofs, being seen of them forty days, and speaking of the things pertaining to THE KINGDOM OF GOD ... When they therefore were come together, they asked of Him, saying, Lord, wilt thou at this time *restore again the kingdom to Israel?* And He said unto them, It is not for you to know the times or the seasons, which the Father hath put in His own power. But ye shall receive power, after that the Holy Ghost is come upon you: and ye shall be witnesses unto Me both in Jerusalem, and in all Judæa, and in Samaria, and UNTO THE UTTERMOST PART OF THE EARTH ".[12]

Notice to whom these words were spoken. It was to " the apostles whom He had chosen ", the Twelve Apostles, and they were to be " witnesses unto [Him] . . . unto the *uttermost part of the earth* ". The uttermost part of the earth in a north-westerly direction from Jerusalem is the BRITISH ISLES.

What happened to the Twelve Apostles and, we might ask especially, what happened to Peter? The *Daily Telegraph* magazine recently reported:

" A mouse, a workman who scratched a message on a wall with a sharp nail, and a woman professor who wouldn't take no for an answer, have contributed to a solution of one of the most intriguing mysteries of the Christian world—positive identification of the bones of St. Peter.

" This is of momentous significance, for the tomb and bones were right under the Altar of the Confession in St. Peter's basilica in Rome.

The claim of the Roman Catholic Church to be the only true one and the claim of the Pope to be Christ's Vicar on earth are to a great extent based on the assumption that St. Peter went to Rome, and was the first Roman Pontiff. The tradition that the First of the Apostles was also the first Bishop of Rome was an inducement of the scattered early Christian communities of the East to accept the Roman supremacy. It was the belief that Peter was crucified in Nero's Circus and buried on the Vatican hill that gave to Rome the character of a city sacred to Christianity" (*Number 250, July 25th, 1969*).

But Peter was never at Rome! There is not the slightest evidence of his ever having been there. He is not mentioned among the brethren whom Paul greets at Rome,[13] a significant omission, and when Paul eventually reached that city and " called the chief of the Jews together ",[14] " They said unto him, we neither received letters out of Judæa concerning thee, neither any of the brethren that came shewed or spake any harm of thee. But we desire to hear of thee what thou thinkest: for as concerning this sect, we know that every where it is spoken against ".[15] Evidently there had been no *public* ministry of the gospel in Rome at this time, A.D. 63. " And when they had appointed him a day, there came many to him into his lodging; to whom he expounded and testified the kingdom of God, persuading them concerning Jesus, both out of the law of Moses, and out of the prophets, from morning till evening ".[16] If the people at Rome had already been visited by Peter *they would not have made this enquiry of Paul.*

What the Bible does tell us is that Peter was used to bring the household of Cornelius—a *Gentile* household—to Christ,[17] and that he and John were present at the first Church Council held in Jerusalem.[18] We also know that he was for some time at Babylon since he wrote his letters from that city.[19] But apart from this brief information the Bible tells us nothing of Peter's later years. However, the Greek historian Metaphrastes informs us:

" Peter was not only in these western [Mediterranean] parts but particularly . . . he was a long time in Britain, where he converted many nations to the faith " (*Cave, Antiquitates Apostolicæ, page 45*).

Yes, the Apostle Peter preached the gospel in Britain, and no less a person than the Venerable Bede (670-735), a Roman Catholic and foremost historian of his day, who wrote *The Ecclesiastical History of the English Nation*, tells us that in A.D. 665 Pope Vitalian sent the relics, i.e. the mortal remains, of Peter and Paul to Oswy, King of Britain:

" However, we have ordered the blessed gifts of the holy martyrs, that is, the relics of the blessed apostles, Peter and Paul, and of the holy martyrs, Laurentius, John, and Paul, and Gregory, and Pancratius, to be delivered to the bearers of these our letters, to be by them delivered to you " (*J. M. Dent, Everyman's Edn., pp. 159-160*).

This report of the final resting place of Peter and Paul is carefully avoided by the Roman Catholic Church! Who, then, is buried under the altar in St. Peter's basilica in Rome? The very latest evidence substantiates the claim to there being an important burial there—precious woollen material, dyed purple and threaded with gold, and graffiti scratched upon the wall inside the recess where the bones were found. But it was not Peter who was buried there but another Peter, masquerading as the Apostle of Christ. He was Simon Magus who established a counterfeit church, imposing the pagan rites of the Babylonian Mystery Religion[20] upon a superficial veneer of Christianity. That church has come down to us today as the Roman Catholic Church: write for our FREE article, Mystery Babylon the Great.

This Simon Magus is described for us in the Bible as one who "used sorcery, and bewitched the people of Samaria, giving out that himself was some great one: to whom they all gave heed, from the least to the greatest, saying, This man is the great power of God. And to him they had regard, because that of long time he had bewitched them with sorceries".[21] It was this man who, "when [he] saw that through laying on of the apostles' hands the Holy Ghost was given . . . offered them money, saying, Give me also this power, that on whomsoever I lay hands, he may receive the Holy Ghost. But Peter said unto him, Thy money perish with thee, because thou hast thought that the gift of God may be purchased with money. Thou hast neither part nor lot in this matter: for thy heart is not right in the sight of God ".[22]

This Simon later appeared at Rome where he impersonated Simon Peter and millions have been deceived ever since, but the real Peter preached the gospel in Britain.

Here a word of explanation may not be out of place. Throughout this book we shall speak of Peter rather than Saint Peter, and Paul rather than Saint Paul. We may learn so much from the life and example of those whom God has used down the ages, but we sometimes forget that they were ORDINARY people serving an EXTRAORDINARY GOD! The Bible says, " Elias [Elijah] was a man subject to like passions as we are, and he PRAYED ".[23] All who accept the Lord Jesus Christ as their own personal Saviour are " called to be saints ",[24] i.e. sanctified and set apart to the service of God. Paul writes to the saints at Rome,[25] Jerusalem,[26] Corinth,[27] Ephesus,[28] Philippi[29] and Colosse.[30] Many, we trust, will be the saints who will read and study this book! And, curiously, while we have been engaged in writing these chapters, the announcement has come over the radio that the Pope has downgraded more than forty ' saints ', including England's St. George, from the liturgical calendar!

THE CROSS AT GLASTONBURY

The inscription reads, "The Cross, the symbol of our faith, the gift of Queen Elizabeth II, marks a Christian sanctuary so ancient that only legend can record its origin".

WINDOW IN ST. JOHN'S CHURCH, GLASTONBURY

The window in the North transept of St. John's Church, Glastonbury, depicts, from left to right, Joseph of Arimathæa, Aristobulus, Simon Zelotes and King Arviragus.

Peter preached in Britain. What of the other Apostles?

Andrew, Simon Peter's brother, preached in Scythia from whence come the Scots. There is even a tradition in Scotland that Andrew once preached the gospel there, and St. Andrew is the patron saint of Scotland to this day.

James, the brother of John, was murdered by Herod. " Now about that time [A.D. 41] Herod the king stretched forth his hands to vex certain of the church. And he killed James the brother of John with the sword ".[31]

John preached in Gaul (modern France). He was banished in later life to the island of Patmos where he wrote the Book of Revelation.[32]

Philip preached in Scythia and Asia Minor.

Bartholomew, possibly another name for Nathanael,[33] ministered in Parthia (modern Persia), and also in Armenia and Upper Phrygia.

Thomas preached in Parthia and north-west India.

Matthew, also known as Levi,[34] preached in Parthia and Æthiopia, according to Metaphrastes.

James the son of Alphæus preached the gospel in Spain and probably Britain:

"The Spanish writers generally contend, after the death of Stephen he (James) came to these western parts, and particularly into Spain (some add Britain and Ireland) where he planted Christianity" (Cave, Antiquitates Apostolicæ, page 148).

Lebbæus Thaddæus, also known as Jude or Judas,[35] ministered in Assyria and Mesopotamia.

Simon the Canaanite, also known as " Simon called Zelotes ",[36] also came to Britain and was martyred here:

"[Simon] directed his journey toward Egypt, then to Cyrene, and Africa . . . and throughout Mauritania and all Libya, preaching the Gospel . . . nor could the coldness of the climate benumb his zeal, or hinder him from whipping himself and the Christian doctrine over to the western islands, yea, even to Britain itself . . . He went at last into Britain, and . . . was crucified . . . and buried there" (Cave, Antiquitates Apostolicæ, page 203).

So here we have the incredible record of history that Peter, Paul, possibly Andrew, probably James, and certainly Simon Zelotes, *all preached the gospel in Britain*, while the remaining Apostles *all preached to people whose descendants are now known in succeeding centuries to have populated these islands*. Eusebius (260-340), the Church's first great historian, tells us simply:

"The Apostles passed beyond the ocean to the isles called the Britannic Isles" (De Demonstratione Evangelii, Lib. III).

But before the Apostles had reached these shores, Philip had sent Joseph of Arimathæa to preach the gospel in Britain. His story we take up in the following Chapter.

1 Proverbs 29: 18
2 Matthew 10: 1-7
3 Matthew 15: 24
4 2 Kings 17: 6
5 2 Kings 17: 23
6 Isaiah 63: 19 (R.V.)
7 2 Samuel 7: 10
8 Isaiah 43: 1
9 Isaiah 43: 10
10 James 1: 1
11 1 Peter 1: 1
12 Acts 1: 1-8

13 Romans 16: 3-15
14 Acts 28: 17
15 Acts 28: 21-22
16 Acts 28: 23
17 Acts 10: 10-48
18 Acts 15: 1-11
19 1 Peter 5: 13
20 Revelation 17: 5
21 Acts 8: 9-11
22 Acts 8: 18-21
23 James 5: 17
24 1 Corinthians 1: 2

25 Romans 1: 7
26 Romans 15: 26
27 2 Corinthians 1: 1
28 Ephesians 1: 1
29 Philippians 1: 1
30 Colossians 1: 2
31 Acts 12: 1-2
32 Revelation 1: 9
33 John 1: 45
34 Mark 2: 14
35 John 14: 22
36 Luke 6: 15

The *Illustrated Bible Geography and Atlas,* containing coloured maps clearly showing the division of Canaan among the Twelve Tribes, and the later Kingdoms of Judah and Israel, will be found most helpful. Copies price 2/6d. (plus 6d. postage) may be purchased from the address at the back of this book. The *Atlas* also contains much other useful information, a Biblical Gazeteer, and 15 colour photographs of the Holy Land.

CHAPTER TWO

JOSEPH OF ARIMATHÆA AT GLASTONBURY

NOT only do the Twelve Apostles vanish from the Scripture record but the Bible is also strangely silent concerning what happened to Joseph of Arimathæa, the rich man mentioned in all four Gospels, who buried the Lord in his own new tomb.

Matthew states, " When the even was come, there came a rich man of Arimathæa, named Joseph, who also himself was Jesus' disciple: he went to Pilate, and begged the body of Jesus. Then Pilate commanded the body to be delivered. And when Joseph had taken the body, he wrapped it in a clean linen cloth, and laid it in his own new tomb, which he had hewn out in the rock: and he rolled a great stone to the door of the sepulchre, and departed ".[1]

Mark tells us, " And now when the even was come, because it was the preparation, that is, the day before the Sabbath, Joseph of Arimathæa, an honourable counsellor, which also waited for the kingdom of God, came, and went in boldly unto Pilate, and craved the body of Jesus. And . . . he gave the body to Joseph. And he bought fine linen, and took Him down, and wrapped Him in the linen, and laid Him in a sepulchre which was hewn out of a rock, and rolled a stone unto the door of the sepulchre ".[2]

Luke's record reads, " And, behold, there was a man named Joseph, a counsellor; and he was a good man, and a just: (the same had not consented to the counsel and deed of them;) he was of Arimathæa, a city of the Jews: who also himself waited for the kingdom of God. This man went unto Pilate, and begged the body of Jesus. And he took it down, and wrapped it in linen, and laid it in a sepulchre that was hewn in stone, wherein never man before was laid ".[3]

Finally, John says, " And after this Joseph of Arimathæa,

15

being a disciple of Jesus, but secretly for fear of the Jews, besought Pilate that he might take away the body of Jesus: and Pilate gave him leave. He came therefore, and took the body of Jesus ".[4]

Thus was the prophecy fulfilled of Jesus that " He made His grave with the wicked, and with the rich in His death."[5] It was prophesied that Jesus should be buried in the tomb of a rich man, and it was Joseph of Arimathæa who was to fulfil that prophecy. The Bible says that Joseph " begged the body of Jesus . . . and laid it in his own new tomb."

Who was this man Joseph of Arimathæa? The Bible indicates that he was a man of social distinction and official rank, for he was " an honourable counsellor ". It also tells us that he was a good and just man and he was rich. Moreover we are told that he " had not consented to the counsel and deed of them " so that he was evidently a member of the Sanhedrin. More explicitly it tells us that " himself waited for the kingdom of God " and that he was " a disciple of Jesus, but secretly for fear of the Jews ".

It must have taken real courage then for Joseph to approach Pilate. Consider for one moment. Having been treacherously betrayed, Jesus had been taken by the priest's guard which had no powers of arrest and had then been illegally tried after dark. After all the evidence had been heard, Caiaphas had taken upon himself to conduct a vicious cross-examination of the prisoner, finally demanding that Jesus be tried in the morning before the Roman governor of Palestine, Pontius Pilate, on a false charge of treason. (Remember, Palestine was at this time part of the Roman Empire. The Jews had no jurisdiction in such matters and only the Roman governor had the power to condemn a man to death.) Pilate had given way to the demand of the mob howling for Jesus' death and had—literally—washed his hands of the affair, thus condemning Jesus to the ignominious death of a criminal. Such was the wickedness of those who would destroy Jesus, and such the suffering of Him who " poured out His soul unto death: [who] was numbered with the transgressors ",[6] and whom God " made . . . to be sin for us, who knew no sin ".[7]

So Joseph " went in boldly unto Pilate and craved the body of Jesus . . . and [Pilate] gave the body to Joseph ". This is strange. One can scarcely believe that Jesus' enemies would have been willing for His body to be taken down and privately buried and for His tomb to become the shrine of a martyr. The fact that Joseph obtained his request would seem to indicate that he had some rightful claim to the body of Jesus which would only be the case *if he were a relative.* And this seems to be the case, for the Jewish Talmud describes Joseph of Arimathæa as being the younger brother of the father of the virgin Mary, in other words, *Joseph of Arimathæa was Jesus' great-uncle.*

Now, strangely, the Bible has nothing further to say about Joseph following the Crucifixion. *What would have been Joseph's reaction when on the third day the stone was rolled away from the tomb and the grave was empty?* Surely this man who was waiting for the Kingdom of God, who was a disciple of Jesus, but secretly for fear of the Jews, who had shown rare courage in begging the body of Jesus, now became the close follower of our Lord. Yet the Bible never mentions him again.

For the disciples of Jesus the transforming experience came at Pentecost. " And when the day of Pentecost was fully come, they were all with one accord in one place. And suddenly there came a sound from heaven as of a rushing mighty wind, and it filled all the house where they were sitting. And there appeared unto them cloven tongues like as of fire, and it sat upon each of them. And they were all filled with the Holy Ghost, and began to speak with other tongues, as the Spirit gave them utterance ".[8]

Immediately after Pentecost there began a great persecution of the Church. Those who had hounded Christ to His death now directed their fury against Jesus' disciples. The Bible records the death of the Church's first martyr—Stephen—and then tells us, " And at that time there was a great persecution against the church which was at Jerusalem; and they were all scattered abroad throughout the regions of Judæa and Samaria, except the apostles. And devout men carried Stephen to his burial, and made great lamentation over him. As for Saul, he made havock of the church, entering into every house, and haling men and women committed them to prison. Therefore they that were scattered abroad went every where preaching the word ".[9]

But where was Joseph? Traditions of great antiquity tell us that JOSEPH OF ARIMATHÆA BROUGHT THE GOSPEL TO BRITAIN within a very few years of the Crucifixion. In fact, there is reason to believe that Joseph was already familiar with the British Isles long before he became a disciple of Jesus. The Latin Vulgate renders " honourable counsellor " as *nobilis decurio.* 'Decurio' was the name given to a town counsellor and also to an officer in the Roman Army. But since one Dr. C. R. Davey Biggs wrote in a little booklet *Ictis and Avalon* that the officer in charge of a tin mine was also called a decurio, there has been much speculation as to the possibility that Joseph of Arimathæa was involved in tin-mining. This would certainly explain the source of Joseph's wealth referred to in the Bible.

But what makes the possibility even more interesting is the fact that there has long been a tradition in the tin-mining area of South-western England that " Joseph was in the trade ". If so, then it may be said with certainty that Joseph would have come to Britain, and probably not once but many times. Britain was the main source of tin. The British Isles were referred to by classical writers as the Cassiterides—tin-bearing islands. In fact, while we have been at work on this book it has been announced that more tin mines are to be opened in Cornwall. The *Sunday Telegraph*, 21st September, 1969, has said, " There is still probably as much tin under the Cornish ground as ever came out of it ". How then did Joseph of Arimathæa come to return to this land with which he was already familiar, not as a merchant of tin but as a messenger of the Cross?

Tradition tells us that at this time of great persecution Joseph of Arimathæa and eleven others were cast adrift from Joppa in an open boat, and that they drifted across the Mediterranean to Marseilles. We find this account recorded by Cardinal Baronius, the 16th century Roman Catholic historian, who spent thirty years writing his *Annales Ecclesiastice*, and had access to the archives of the Vatican Library. Baronius states that it was in the year A.D. 35 that Joseph of Arimathæa, Lazarus[10] (whom Jesus raised from the dead and whom the Jews sought to kill[11]), Mary and Martha, Lazarus's sisters, also Marcella their maid, and Maximin a disciple, were put into a boat without sails or oars, and that they eventually came to Marseilles in France and afterwards crossed to Britain.

A glance at the map facing page 61 will show the route travelled by Joseph. His companions are also stated by the poet Mistral to have included Trophimus,[12] Cleon, Eutropius, Restitutus whom we know from the Bible as " the man born blind ",[13] Martial, Saturninus, Mary the wife of Cleophas[14] and Mary Magdalene.[15] Whatever the exact complement of Joseph's party, Lazarus is to this day recognised as having become first Bishop of Marseilles while the names of these other saints are perpetuated in the records of the Gallic Church.

And so Joseph and his little party came to Britain, sailing inland to the Isle of Avalon which we now know as Glastonbury. In those days the sea which is now fourteen miles away came much further inland and lapped the foot of Glastonbury Tor, the 500-foot high hill which dominates the countryside for miles around—see the photograph facing page 21. Joseph is said to have planted his staff in the soil of Wearyall Hill, and there it took root and grew into a thorn tree. Of this thorn tree more will be said later.

Joseph and his companions were met by King Arviragus who granted them tax-free twelve hides of land. A hide is thought to have been 160 acres, so that the total area represented 1,920 acres. We find this Royal Charter recorded in the official archives from that day to this! Domesday Book, published in 1087, tells us of:

"The Domus Dei, in the great monastery of Glastonbury, called the Secret of the Lord. This Glastonbury Church possesses, in its own ville XII hides of land which have never paid tax"

and the twelve hides may still be traced today, as will be seen in the reproduction, facing page 53, of "A Map of the Hundreds of Glaston XII Hides" from Phelps' *The History and Antiquities of Somersetshire*, published in 1836.

This charter of land was often referred to in succeeding centuries whenever disputes arose as to the seniority of the British Church above the claims of Rome. In fact, the primacy of the Church in Britain was never held in question until at the Council of Pisa in 1409 it was disputed by the Ambassadors of France and Spain. It was then contended that the French and Spanish Churches must yield precedence to the British Church as this had been *founded by Joseph of Arimathæa* immediately after the Passion of Christ. This ruling was further upheld by the Councils of Constance 1417, Sienna 1424 and Basle 1434. Archbishop Ussher (1581-1656) states that the basis of this claim was the burial of Joseph of Arimathæa at Glastonbury and *the donation of twelve hides of land.*

Joseph and his companions now erected what must certainly have been the first Christian church above ground. Of course, we know from the Bible that it was the custom for Christians to gather for fellowship in their homes. The Church, the Greek word *ekklesia* meaning the ' called out ones ', was the PEOPLE, not the building. Notice, Paul says, " Greet Priscilla and Aquila . . . likewise . . . the CHURCH that is in their *house* ",[16] " Aquila and Priscilla salute you . . . with the CHURCH that is in their *house* ",[17] " the CHURCH which is in [Nymphas'] *house* ",[18] and " Archippus our fellow-soldier, and . . . the CHURCH in thy *house* ".[19] During the time of intense persecution by the Roman Empire the Christians at Rome met in the catacombs underground. Gradually, the *place* where Christians met became known as the *church* instead of the PEOPLE.

So here, if the tradition be true, we have Joseph and his companions constructing the first church building above ground. It was made from wattles daubed with mud, and was thatched with reeds, and when completed it measured sixty feet long and twenty-six feet wide, approximately the same dimensions as the Tabernacle in the wilderness.[20]

For hundreds of years this sacred building was preserved. In the year 630 Paulinus encased it in lead and built over it a beautiful chapel. Unhappily, in 1184 there was a disastrous fire, and the little Wattle Church was completely destroyed. However, a Norman chapel was built over the same spot immediately afterwards and, though ruined, this remains today. Thus we can say with reasonable certainty that St. Joseph's Chapel at Glastonbury Abbey stands today exactly where the Wattle Church was erected only a few years after the Resurrection, and where Joseph himself was buried. John Leland tells us, quoting Maelgwyn of Avalon's *Historia de Rebus Britannicis*, written about A.D. 540:

"The Isle of Avalon greedy of burials . . . received thousands of sleepers, among whom Joseph de Marmore from Aramathea by name, entered his perpetual sleep. And he lies in a bifurcated line next the southern angle of the oratory made of circular wattles by thirteen inhabitants of the place over the powerful adorable Virgin ".

This would suggest that Mary the mother of Jesus was buried at Glastonbury. Is this why, long before such dedications became the custom, St. Joseph's Chapel was also called St. Mary's? And is this why, as will be seen from the photographs on the facing page, there is a stone set in the South wall of the Chapel bearing the simple inscription JESUS MARIA? It is curious that William of Malmesbury in his *Magna Tabula Glastoniæa* refers alike to Joseph as to John[21] as the paranymphos or guardian of Jesus' mother.

The tomb of Joseph was inscribed with a simple epitaph:
"AD BRITANNOS VENI POST CHRISTUM SEPELIVI. DOCUI. QUIEVI ".
Translated this reads:

"I CAME TO BRITAIN AFTER BURYING CHRIST. I TAUGHT. I REST ".

Nothing now remains of Joseph's grave. But there is an empty stone sarcophagus in St. John's Parish Church. There, according to tradition, and in circumstances we have not space to tell, his remains were placed.

And so he who buried Jesus in his own new tomb found a resting place in Britain. The honourable counsellor who in the days of Jesus' earthly life had been His secret disciple was he who brought the gospel to these shores.

It is a wonderful story we have begun to tell!

[1] Matthew 27: 57-60
[2] Mark 15: 42-46
[3] Luke 23: 50-53
[4] John 19: 38
[5] Isaiah 53: 9
[6] Isaiah 53: 12
[7] 2 Corinthians 5: 21
[8] Acts 2: 1-4
[9] Acts 8: 1-4
[10] John 11: 1-46
[11] John 12: 10-11
[12] Acts 20: 4
[13] John 9: 1-38
[14] John 19: 25
[15] Mark 16: 9
[16] Romans 16: 3-5
[17] 1 Corinthians 16: 19
[18] Colossians 4: 15
[19] Philemon 2
[20] Exodus 26: 1-37
[21] John 19: 26-27

JESUS-MARY STONE AT GLASTONBURY

The stone, set in the South wall of St. Joseph's (also known as St. Mary's) Chapel, is said to be one of the stations visited by pilgrims during their tour of the Abbey. The Lombardic lettering is 13th century.

GLASTONBURY TOR
Rising to a height of 521 feet and surmounted by the ruined tower of St. Michael's Church, Glastonbury Tor dominates the landscape for miles around. It was a Druidic 'high place'.

CHAPTER THREE

GLASTONBURY TOR AND THE DRUIDS

GLASTONBURY TOR stands 521 feet above sea level and from its summit one has an uninterrupted view in all directions. On a clear day, it affords a sight of South Wales and the Severn Estuary, the prehistoric camps and beacons of the Mendips and Quantocks, and the hills of Wiltshire and Dorset.

At the top of Glastonbury Tor is a ruined tower, all that remains of St. Michael's Church. A church has stood here since the earliest centuries of the Christian era for St. Patrick is said to have found a ruined church on the summit in the fifth century and to have rebuilt it. The body of this church was destroyed in the earthquake of 1275. It was once again rebuilt, but only the massive tower which was at the West end of the church and was restored in 1804, remains today. However, there is no more inspiring sight in Britain today than the view of Glastonbury Tor and St. Michael's Tower dominating the skyline no matter from which direction one approaches. The conical appearance of the hill bears a strong resemblance to Mount Tabor in Palestine and many a traveller has been thrilled by the sight of it. We may well imagine the reaction of Joseph of Arimathæa as he set his sails toward it.

The church which once stood here was undoubtedly erected on the site of a pre-Christian fire altar. Glastonbury Tor was a Druidic Gorsedd or 'high place' reminding us of the high places of the Old Testament. Here the Druids worshipped the sun. Terraces winding round the Tor may still be observed, and the Tor would have been the site of an astronomical observatory.

It is not uncommon to come across churches placed at the very summit of a hill. The very name 'Churchill' must have come to us from the association of churches with hills, and the reason

21

for this is very simple. As the Christian faith began to supplant the former pagan worship of the Druids—the religious order which dominated Britain in pre-Christian times—so its high places were given over to the worship of Christ. So it must have been with Glastonbury Tor. Where once the Beltane fire flamed from its summit at the spring equinox, now a church was erected in worship of the true " Sun of righteousness . . . with healing in His wings ".[1]

The Bible throws great light on the worship of the pre-Christian Britons. The very existence of these high places not only reveals their pagan idolatry but also shows us that Britain was peopled by Israelite tribes. On page 9 we mentioned briefly that the ten tribes of Israel were carried captive into Assyria, 735-670 B.C. We showed that some of the Apostles, in fulfilling their mission to the lost sheep of the house of Israel,[2] came to the BRITISH ISLES, from which we inferred that the people of Britain were of *Israelite ancestry*. Now here is startling confirmation of that fact. *The worship of pre-Christian Britain and of pre-captivity Israel is almost identical.*

Notice what the Bible says, " And it came to pass on the morrow, that Balak took Balaam, and brought him up into the HIGH PLACES OF BAAL, that thence he might see the utmost part of the people ".[3] Baal was the sun-god whom the children of Israel idolatrously worshipped in the HIGH PLACES!

" And the children of Israel did evil in the sight of the LORD, and served BAALIM: and they forsook the LORD God of their fathers, which brought them out of the land of Egypt, and followed other gods, of the gods of the people that were round about them, and bowed themselves unto them, and provoked the LORD to anger. And they forsook the LORD, and served BAAL and ASHTAROTH [EASTER]. And the anger of the LORD was hot against Israel, and He delivered them into the hands of spoilers that spoiled them, and He sold them into the hands of their enemies round about, so that they could not any longer stand before their enemies ".[4] This was in the days immediately after Joshua, about 1400 B.C. In fact, Israel was already turning to idolatry before they had even entered the promised land.[5]

From 978-938 B.C. Solomon was king over Israel, and it was at this time that the religious life of the nation began to decline. " And [Solomon] had seven hundred wives, princesses, and three hundred concubines: and his wives turned away his heart. For it came to pass, when Solomon was old, that his wives turned away his heart after other gods: and his heart was not perfect with the LORD his God, as was the heart of David his father. For Solomon went after ASHTORETH [EASTER] the goddess of the Zidonians, and after Milcom the abomination of the Ammonites. And Solomon did evil in the sight of the LORD, and went not fully after the LORD, as did David his father. Then did Solomon build an HIGH PLACE for Chemosh, the abomination of Moab, in the HILL that is before Jerusalem, and for Molech, the abomination of the children of Ammon. And likewise did he for all his strange wives, which burnt incense and sacrificed unto their gods ".[6]

The decline which now set in led to the utter corruption of God's Israel people so that in the days of Ahab (874-857 B.C.) a large body of Baalite priests was maintained. "And Ahab the son of Omri did evil in the sight of the LORD above all that were before him. And it came to pass, as if it had been a light thing for him to walk in the sins of Jeroboam the son of Nebat, that he took to wife Jezebel the daughter of Ethbaal king of the Zidonians, and went and served BAAL, and worshipped him. And he reared up an altar for Baal in the house of Baal, which he had built in Samaria. And Ahab made a grove; and Ahab did more to provoke the LORD God of Israel to anger than all the kings of Israel that were before him ".[7] It was at this time that the prophet Elijah was sent to Ahab with the word of the Lord,[8] God answered by fire from heaven,[9] and the prophets of Baal were destroyed.[10]

However, Israel never turned back to God. It was their continued idolatry, their pagan worship of BAAL the sun-god in their HIGH PLACES that precipitated the overthrow of the kingdom in 722 B.C., and their captivity by the Assyrians.

" In the ninth year of Hoshea [king of Israel], the king of Assyria took Samaria, and carried Israel away into Assyria, and placed them in Halah and in Habor by the river of Gozan, and in the cities of the Medes. For so it was, that the children of Israel had sinned against the LORD their God, which had brought them up out of the land of Egypt, from under the hand of Pharoah king of Egypt, and had feared other gods, and walked in the statutes of the heathen, whom the LORD cast out from before the children of Israel, and of the kings of Israel, which they had made. And the children of Israel did secretly those things that were not right against the LORD their God, and they built them HIGH PLACES in all their cities, from the tower of the watchmen to the fenced city. And they set them up images and groves in every HIGH HILL, and under every green tree: and there they burnt incense in all the HIGH PLACES, as did the heathen whom the LORD carried away before them; and wrought wicked things to provoke the LORD to anger: for they served idols, whereof the LORD had said unto them, Ye shall not do this thing . . . And they left all the commandments of the LORD their God, and made them molten images, even two calves, and made a grove, and worshipped all the host of heaven, and served BAAL. And they caused their sons and their daughters to pass through the fire, and used divination and enchantments, and sold themselves to do evil in the sight of the LORD, to provoke Him to anger. Therefore the LORD was very angry with Israel, and removed them out of His sight: there was none left but the tribe of Judah only ".[11]

Rev. F. W. Gotch, LL.D., in Smith's *Dictionary of the Bible,* tells us:

" The worship of Baal amongst the [Israelites] appears to have been appointed with much pomp and ceremonial. Temples were erected to him;[12] his images were set up;[13] his altars were very numerous.[14] were erected particularly on lofty eminences,[15] on the roofs of houses;[16] there were priests in great numbers.[17] and of various classes;[18] the worshippers appear to have been arrayed in appropriate robes;[19] the worship was performed by burning incense[20] and offering burnt sacrifices, which occasionally consisted of human victims.[21] The officiating priests danced with frantic shouts around the altar, and cut themselves with knives to excite the attention and compassion of the god "[22] *(1863 Edn., Vol. I, page 145).*

Yet the worship of Molech was even more inhuman and revolting. It appears that there were purifications and ordeals by fire, mutilation, vows of perpetual celibacy and virginity, and even human sacrifices. Such was the depravity of Israel at this time. The Bible tells us that children were sacrificed by burning, " And they have built the HIGH PLACES of Tophet . . . to burn their sons and their daughters in the fire ".[23]

These then were the people who in the centuries following the captivity by Assyria came to Britain and established the Druidic worship.

Now we can understand the great similarity, in many respects, between the Old Testament faith and the Druidic religion of Western Europe and the British Isles. The Druidic faith greatly resembles the idolatrous worship of ten-tribed Israel at the time of their captivity; clearly this must have been its origin.

It is sometimes stated that as a result of the Assyrian captivity, Israel reformed and reverted to the pure worship of their fathers, but under whose influence? There was no one to teach them. Hosea, some years before the captivity, prophesied, " For the children of Israel shall abide many days without a king, and without a prince, and without a sacrifice, and without an image, and without an ephod, and without teraphim ".[24] There was no king, prophet or priest to point the way back to God. Yet if such a wholesale conversion had been possible there would still have been need for Christ's substitutionary death and sacrifice. His Resurrection and Ascension, the outpouring of the Holy Spirit, and the inauguration of the New Covenant.

However, the Bible specifically states that the captive tribes profaned the Lord's name among the heathen. " Moreover the word of the LORD came unto me, saying, Son of man, when the house of Israel dwelt in their own land, they defiled it by their own way and by their doings . . . wherefore I poured My fury upon them for the blood that they had shed upon the land, and for their idols wherewith they had polluted it: and I scattered them among the heathen, and they were dispersed through the countries: according to their way and according to their doings I judged them. And when they entered unto the heathen, whither they went, THEY PROFANED MY HOLY NAME, when they said to them, *These are the people of the Lord, and are gone forth out of His land.* But I had pity for Mine holy name, which the house of Israel had profaned among the heathen, whither they went. Therefore say unto the house of Israel, Thus saith the Lord GOD; I do not this for your sakes, O house of Israel, but for Mine holy name's sake, which ye have profaned among the heathen, whither ye went. And I will sanctify My great name, which was profaned among the heathen, which ye have profaned in the midst of them; and the heathen shall know that I am the LORD, saith the Lord GOD, when I shall be sanctified in you before their eyes ".[25]

Notice that this prophecy is to the house of Israel, the ten tribes who were taken captive into Assyria and never returned. Notice that the Lord says, " I . . . will bring you into your own land " and that then " the heathen shall know that I am the LORD . . . when I shall be sanctified in you before their eyes ". This was fulfilled when, in the centuries following the Assyrian captivity, the tribes of Israel moved into their new land, the " appointed place ",[26] the Isles of the sea[27] in the north and west,[28] where they nationally embraced the faith of Christ, and became His witnesses throughout the earth.[29] (Of course, a far greater fulfilment of this prophecy has yet to take place.[30])

So, in the centuries before Christ, the tribes of Israel migrated through Europe to the British Isles bringing with them their idolatrous worship which today is described as Druidism. Notice this quotation from the *Official Guide Book to Stonehenge* produced by the Ministry of Public Building and Works, and published by Her Majesty's Stationery Office:

" The ancient Druids had no connection with Stonehenge or any other monument of the Bronze Age or indeed of any earlier period in the British Isles. No doubt they pretended they had, or even that they built it. They were a class of people who no doubt had a good deal of knowledge; they came to Britain during the early Iron Age invasions in about the third century before Christ " (*Page 20*).

The claim that the Druids " had a good deal of knowledge " is an understatement, as we shall see. However, the statement that the Druids came to Britain in the third century before Christ accords well with our observation that the Druidic religion closely resembles Israelite idolatry as described in the Bible.

Lest we convey a false impression as to the inhabitants of these Isles in the pre-Christian era, we hasten to add that there still remained much in the Druidic religion which was noble and fine and in harmony with the Old Testament faith. Such innovations as there had been were made gradually and in such a way as not to give offence. It was not that the worship of the true God was ever proscribed; rather the worship of other gods was added in such a way that the outward form of religion was little changed. It was a religion of compromise in which much that had seemed harsh and severe under the Mosaic Law was watered down, and there was less reproof of sin. Perhaps one might say that Druidism bore the same relationship to the faith of the Old Testament as does modern ' Christianity ' to the faith of the New Testament. Israel took to worshipping the sun in much the same way that Christians today observe pagan festivals such as Christmas and Easter for which there is no scriptural authority but which are mistakenly supposed to enjoy the divine approval. No doubt people then, as now, were more concerned with the outward forms of worship than its true object.

Druidism then was the religion of pre-Christian Britain and much of Western Europe. Its most learned priests, bards and philosophers lived in Britain, and since their doctrine could never be committed to writing, foreigners were compelled to come to Britain to be initiated into its rites. There seem to have been various Druidic orders. One class was concerned strictly with the priestly or sacrificial office. There was another class which were considered prophets and were occasionally employed at the altar, but with a special duty of the composition of music and sacred hymns. A third strictly secular class was occupied in composing and reciting poetry for the encouragement of virtue and the condemnation of vice. A fourth class was devoted to astrology, sorcery, and occultism. The priesthood was hereditary but the chief Druid was elected.

All this reminds us of the religious orders of God's Israel people in the Old Testament. There was the High Priest[31] who presided over the Temple ceremonies, a course of officiating priests,[32] then the Levites[33] who were the musicians and singers, and also the prophets who fulfilled a secular as well as a religious office through their " schools of the prophets ".

There were many Druid temples in Britain and the Druids lived in fraternities in the vicinity of the Temple where they officiated. Other Druids were engaged in public and secular activities and served in the families of the nobility; certainly they were important and influential people. They were exempt from taxation and from military service. All this reminds us of the Levitical priesthood.

The Druids were therefore ministers of religion, poets, musicians and philosophers. They were also great legislators and teachers, and their motto is said to have been, " the truth against the world ". This may account for the origin of the word ' Druid ' from *druthin*—servant of truth, or perhaps, as seems more likely, from *drus* meaning an oak tree.

Thus we have a great amount of evidence showing the close relationship between Druidism and the faith of the Old Testament. Each had a High Priest with a breastplate that was almost identical. Each had a priesthood that was similar, and was exempt from taxation and military service. Both religions taught the Mosaic record of the Creation, of the fall of man, and of the coming of the Messiah.

Then compare Druidism with the corrupt religion of Israel at the time of the Assyrian captivity. Both worshipped Baal, built temples to him in the groves, by the oak trees, and on lofty hills. Both stained their altars with human blood. The British Druids even used the magic wand, apparently an imitation of Aaron's rod which budded,[34] and of Moses' rod[35] by which great miracles were wrought.

Look at the definition of ' Druid ' as given in Webster's *Third New International Dictionary* :

DRUID.—A member of a priesthood in ancient Gaul, Britain and Ireland who are said to have studied the natural sciences, prophesied through priestly sacrifices, and acted as judges and teachers, but who later appeared in Irish and Welsh sagas and Christian legends as magicians and wizards.

This definition is an apt description of the religious life of Israel as it must have been in the centuries following their captivity in Assyria, while Gaul, Britain and France are specifically stated by ancient writers to have been among the places to which the tribes migrated.

Space precludes our treatment of the subject as we might have wished. It is believed, for instance, that Hu Gadarn, also known as Hu the Mighty, led a contingent of Hebrew people to these shores about 1800 B.C. If so, it is easy to believe that he introduced the patriarchal faith which at last was submerged in Druidism with the coming of the Celts. But of this for the moment the writer has no proof.

These then are the people to whom Joseph came, who lived in Britain at the time of Christ. It has been suggested that the similarity between Druidism and the faith of Israel in the Old Testament made the British people especially responsive to the gospel message. In particular, it has been pointed out that the Druids believed in the immortality of the soul—Julius Caesar said it was the strength of British resistance—but notice what the Bible says:

" And the LORD God formed man of the dust of the ground, and breathed into his nostrils the breath of life; and man *became* a living SOUL."[36]

" Shall MORTAL man be more just than God?"[37]

" The SOUL that sinneth, it shall *die.*"[38]

" The wages of sin is *death.*"[39]

" For all have sinned."[40]

" [Christ] *only* hath IMMORTALITY."[41]

" Our Saviour Jesus Christ . . . hath abolished death, and hath brought life and IMMORTALITY to light through the gospel."[42]

Job said, " For I know that my Redeemer liveth, and that He shall stand at the latter day upon the earth: and though after my skin worms destroy this body, yet *in my flesh* shall I see God."[43]

Jesus said, " I am the RESURRECTION, and the life: he that believeth in Me, though he were dead, yet shall he live."[44]

The Bible teaches not that man has a soul but that he *is* a soul. It shows us that souls can die. It tells us that Christ alone has immortality. It offers us the hope of RESURRECTION and of ETERNAL LIFE in Christ's coming kingdom upon earth.

" For the wages of sin is death; but the gift of God is ETERNAL LIFE through Jesus Christ our Lord."[45]

May YOU receive Christ's gift of eternal life today!

[1] Malachi 4: 2	[16] Jeremiah 32: 29	[31] Exodus 28: 1
[2] Matthew 10: 6	[17] 1 Kings 18: 19	[32] 2 Chronicles 7: 6
[3] Numbers 22: 41	[18] 2 Kings 10: 19	[33] Numbers 8: 5-26
[4] Judges 2: 11-14	[19] 2 Kings 10: 22	[34] Numbers 17: 8
[5] Joshua 24: 14, 23	[20] Jeremiah 7: 9	[35] Exodus 4: 17
[6] 1 Kings 11: 3-8	[21] Jeremiah 19: 5	[36] Genesis 2: 7
[7] 1 Kings 16: 30-33	[22] 1 Kings 18: 26-28	[37] Job 4: 17
[8] 1 Kings 18: 1-2	[23] Jeremiah 7: 31	[38] Ezekiel 18: 4
[9] 1 Kings 18: 38	[24] Hosea 3: 4	[39] Romans 6: 23
[10] 1 Kings 18: 40	[25] Ezekiel 36: 16-23	[40] Romans 3: 23
[11] 2 Kings 17: 6-18	[26] 2 Samuel 7: 10	[41] 1 Timothy 6: 16
[12] 2 Kings 11: 18	[27] Isaiah 24: 15	[42] 2 Timothy 1: 10
[13] 2 Kings 10: 26	[28] Isaiah 49: 12	[43] Job 19: 25-26
[14] Jeremiah 11: 13	[29] Isaiah 43: 10-12	[44] John 11: 25
[15] 1 Kings 18: 20	[30] Jeremiah 31: 31-34	[45] Romans 6: 23

CHALICE WELL GARDEN

In the distance, Glastonbury Tor and the ruined tower of St. Michael's Church.

CHALICE WELL

The spring, rising from the slope of Chalice Hill, pours forth 25,000 gallons of water per day and has never been known to fail. Here most probably took place the first Christian baptisms in Britain.

CHAPTER FOUR

CHALICE WELL AND THE SOMERSET ZODIAC

I AM writing this in a corner of the delightful gardens of the Chalice Well at Glastonbury. A few yards in front of where I am sitting is the famous well covered over today by the lid bearing a symbolic design that was made for it fifty years ago. Below me and to my right the garden slopes away, a blaze of colour with wall-flowers and forget-me-nots, aubretias and tulips, and a flowering cherry tree. A couple of trees sprung from the Glastonbury Thorn are in full flower. A little to my left are two yew trees, and I am reminded that in 1961, quite close to this well, the stump of a yew tree was found twelve feet below the present ground level: scientific examination showed it to have been alive in A.D. 300. Through the branches of the yew trees I can see the Tor with St. Michael's tower outlined against the sky, while Chalice Hill rises up behind me.

This is a beautiful spot. The heavy rain earlier in the day has given way to brilliant sunshine. All around the air is filled with birdsong, pigeons cooing in the trees, a blackbird chinking a little way off, and a thrush is singing in the distance. A brimstone yellow butterfly has flitted across the path and cabbage-whites flutter among the flowers, and the slight breeze wafts a lovely fragrance from the mass of flowers. At this moment it is hard to think of a more delightful spot.

Just out of sight, a little lower down the garden, the water gushes out of a pipe, flowing down a little channel and into a pool, and colouring the stone red from its iron content. The spring which feeds the well rises on the slope of Chalice Hill and pours forth 25,000 gallons of water per day. It has been doing so for thousands of years and has never been known to fail. In 1921 and 1922 it was this spring and Chalice Well that saved the little town of Glastonbury from drought.

It was here at the foot of the Tor and around this well that Joseph of Arimathæa and his companions must have built their wattle huts more than nineteen hundred years ago, and here, we believe, a Christian settlement continued until about A.D. 400 when Patrick instituted the monastic life on a site adjacent to the Wattle Church eight hundred yards away. Those early settlers and those who took their place were called anchorites, and the name was perpetuated in the Anchor Inn, an early building in the vicinity of the well. William of Malmesbury (1080-1143) mentions the well and here, if his record is to be accepted, the first Christian baptisms were held, and King Lucius, who did so much to spread the faith after the initial flush of enthusiasm had died away, was himself baptised.

King Lucius, also known as Llewrug Mawr, was the grandson of Cyllinus and the great-grandson of Caratacus whom we shall write about later (see page 46). He was king towards the end of the 2nd century and is said to have sent emissaries to Eleutherius, the Bishop of Rome, with the request that missionaries be sent to Britain. Eleutherius sent four missionaries, Dyfan and Fagan and Medwy and Elfan (or it may have been that he sent only two, Medwy and Elfan being the returned British emissaries), and the date of their mission was probably A.D. 183.

William of Malmesbury in his *Antiquities of Glastonbury* tells how these missionaries journeyed through Britain and came to Glastonbury:

" There, God leading them, they found an old church built, as 'twas said, by the hands of Christ's disciples, and prepared by God Himself for the salvation of souls, which Church the Heavenly Builder Himself showed to be consecrated by many miraculous deeds, and many mysteries of healing . . . And they afterwards pondered the Heavenly message that the Lord had specially chosen this spot before all the rest of Britain as the place where His Mother's name might be invoked. They also found the whole story in ancient writings, how the Holy Apostles, having been scattered throughout the world, St. Philip coming into France with a host of disciples sent twelve of them into Britain to preach, and that there, taught by revelation they constructed the said chapel which the Son of God afterwards dedicated to the honour of His Mother; and, that to these same twelve, three kings, pagan though they were, gave twelve portions of land for their sustenance. Moreover, they found a written record of their doings, and on that account they loved this spot above all others, and they also, in memory of the first twelve chose twelve of their own, and made them live on the island with the approval of King Lucius. These twelve thereafter abode there in divers spots as anchorites—in the same spots, indeed, which the first twelve inhabited. Yet they used to meet together continuously in the Old Church in order to celebrate Divine worship more devoutly, just as the three pagan kings had long ago granted the said island with its surroundings to the twelve former disciples of Christ, so the said Phagan and Deruvian [Fagan and Dyfan] obtained it from King Lucius for these their twelve companions and for others to follow thereafter. And thus, many succeeding these, but always twelve in number, abode in the said island during many years up to the coming of St. Patrick, the apostle of the Irish " (*Chapter II*).

Lucius is mentioned by many other authorities, including Bede (670-735) who tells us in his *Ecclesiastical History of the English Nation :*

" Lucius, king of the Britons, sent a letter to [Eleutherius], entreating that by his command he might be made a Christian. He soon obtained his pious request, and the Britons preserved the faith, which they had received, uncorrupted and entire, in peace and tranquility until the time of the Emperor Diocletian " *(J. M. Dent, Everyman's Edn., page 9).*

It is to King Lucius that the national conversion of Britain to the Christian faith is usually attributed. Four centres of early British Christianity—Glastonbury, London, Llandaff and Gloucester—have traditional associations with him and the story of the Eleutherian mission survives in the names of three churches in Glamorganshire, Llan*fedwy* (i.e. Medwy's), Merthyr *Dyfan* (Dyfan the Martyr), and St. *Fagan's*, also Llan*lleirwg* (Llewrug's or Lucius') Church, now St. Mellon's, near Cardiff.

The association of King Lucius with London has come down to us through the Church of St. Peter's, Cornhill, which claims to be London's oldest church foundation, the first seat of the Bishops of that city, and founded by King Lucius himself. There was a plate in the vestry of the church which read :

" Bee it known to all mèn that in the year of Our Lord God 179 Lucives, the first Christian king of this land, then called Britaine, founded ye first Church in London, that is to say, ye Church of St. Peter-Upon-Cornehill and hee founded there an Archbishop's See and made that Church ye Metropolitane and Chiefe Church of this kingdome and so it endured ye space of 400 years and more, unto the coming of St. Avstin thè Apostle of England, the which was sent into this land by St. Gregorie, ye Doctor of ye Church, in the Time of King Ethelbert and then was the Archbishop's See and Pall removed from yè said Church of St. Peter-Upon-Cornehill unto Dorobernia that now is called Canterburie and there it remaineth to this day and Millet, a monke which came into this land with St. Avstin, hee was made the first Bishop of London and his Seè was in St. Paul's Church and this Lucives king was the first founder of St Peter's Church-Upon-Cornehill and hee reigned king in this land after Brute [Brutus of Troy] 1245 yeares and in the year of Our Lord God 124 Lucives was crowned king and hee was buried (After some Chronicles hee was buried at Gloucester in that Place where ye order of St. Francis standeth now)."

This plate was put up after the Great Fire of London in 1666 and is a modernised translation of a much older plate, which is quoted by Archbishop Ussher (1581-1656) and must have been put up between 1268 and 1313. (The ' Place where ye order of St. Francis now standeth ' at Gloucester was not founded until 1268, but Ralph de Baldoc, a Bishop of London, mentions a copy of the plate and he died in 1313).

But the name of King Lucius is also associated with Glastonbury Tor as he is reputed to have built a church dedicated to St. Michael at its summit. In the last Chapter we showed that when the Christian faith replaced the former pagan worship, it was the natural thing to erect a church on those 'high places'[1] where formerly pagan rites were practised, and this was what King Lucius did.

No one knows exactly how old Chalice Well is or even how it got its name. The well is evidently of Druidic origin and must have played an integral part in ancient pagan rituals of sunlight and water, with the Tor rising above it as the 'high place' and focal point of a great pagan sanctuary. Today the well shaft is built of massive stones and appears to have been constructed in the early 12th century. That would have been only a few years after the great Abbey fire of 1184 and it must have been constructed to provide an improved water supply to the Abbey.

One of the curious features of the well is the fact that at the foot of the western wall of the well shaft is an archway leading into a pentagonal chamber. The purpose for which this was built we can only speculate at the moment. There is so much that has still to be found out. The stones of the well are even ripple-marked like those of Stonehenge according to Sir Flinders Petrie, and Stonehenge has yet to yield up all its secrets. When some of these questions are answered we shall know a lot more about the origins of this Island race and it will confirm what the revelation of the Bible already tells us.

No one knows for certain how Chalice Well got its name. The name does not appear in any document before the early thirteenth century, and then as 'Chalcwelle', and the entrance to the well is still today in Chilkwell Street. Perhaps it is a corruption of the word chalybeate, i.e. iron-bearing, which describes the mineral content of the water. The water has curative properties and Chalice Well drew enormous crowds of people in the mid-eighteenth century when a certain Matthew Chancellor reported how he had been healed of asthma after drinking a glass of this water on seven successive Sundays. Many other healings were reported and some still are today.

Here, as so often in Glastonbury, history, tradition and romance are inextricably woven together. The usually accepted belief is that Chalice Well derives its name from the chalice or cup of the Lord's Supper[2] which Joseph of Arimathæa is supposed to have brought with him and which he is alleged—for reasons we can only surmise—to have buried in Chalice Hill. But there seems to be no historical foundation for the story, and certain it is that legends of the chalice or graal were current long centuries before the Christian era. In Eastern tradition it was the pagan cup of plenty, the fount of life, health and blessing, and it had its origin in ancient vegetation rites.

However, mention of the chalice or graal naturally brings to mind not only Joseph of Arimathæa but also King Arthur and his Knights of the Round Table. Arthur was a British general who lived in the sixth century and died A.D. 540. He was buried at Glastonbury, his Queen Guinevere beside him, and their tomb was discovered there in 1191. In the coffin was a leaden plate in the form of a cross with the inscription in Latin, *Hic jacet sepultus inclytus Rex Arthurus in Insula Avalonia,* which means, " Here lies interred in the Isle of Avalon the renowned King Arthur ". The remains of King Arthur and Queen Guinevere were re-interred in the Great Church of the Abbey and the fragmentary remains of the shrine were discovered in 1934; this spot is still marked in the turf today.

Camelot, the traditional seat of King Arthur, is now firmly established as South Cadbury, only twelve miles from Glaston-bury. Excavations there in 1967 revealed that a prehistoric ram-part had been refortified in the 5th-6th century for military use. Digging was re-commenced in 1968 and will continue in 1969.

Now in *La Queste del Saint Graal,* we read the following statement concerning King Arthur's Round Table:

" The Round Table was constructed, not without great significance, upon the advice of Merlin. By its name the Round Table is meant to signify the round world and *round canopy of the planets* and the elements in the firmament, where are to be seen the stars and many other things "

and what is truly astonishing is that here in the Somerset country-side, *a huge representation of the Zodiac has been artificially con-structed by means of prehistoric earthworks and water-courses.* This enormous map of the stars modelled against the hills and river beds of Somerset, must have been laid down *nearly 5,000 years ago,* but was only discovered in 1925 when aerial photo-graphs revealed for the first time the huge effigies resembling Zodiacal creatures, arranged in a circle ten miles across and more than thirty miles in diameter. Evidently the reason why we can still trace them is because the land on which they lie was the property of the Abbey, and the monks were scrupulously careful to preserve the ancient landmarks and waterways. But who con-structed the Somerset Zodiac? And who was responsible for Stonehenge?

The Zodiac, by which we mean the apparent path traversed by the planets across the heavens, seems to find its chief connota-tion today in the daily horoscopes published in the newspapers— notice God's condemnation of Babylon with its " astrologers . . . stargazers . . . monthly prognosticators "[3]—but it was not always so. The true spiritual significance of the Zodiac is that it is *the divine plan of the ages written in the stars.*

The writers of the Bible recognised and understood the revelation of God in the heavens. Notice, in the oldest book of the Bible, the Lord asks Job, " Canst thou bind the sweet influences of PLEIADES, or loose the bands of ORION? Canst thou bring forth MAZZAROTH in his season? or canst thou guide ARCTURUS with his sons? "[4] These refer, of course, to well-known star groups. But notice the word *Mazzaroth*. In the margin it is translated " *the twelve signs* " and it means the ZODIAC.

The Zodiac, when correctly interpreted, starting from Virgo the Virgin and ending with Leo the Lion, tells the whole wondrous story of man's creation and redemption. These twelve signs and their supplementary constellations tell us of the setting aside and training of the chosen Israel race, and of its becoming, by the outpouring of the Holy Spirit, the nucleus of the Kingdom of God upon earth. So, though little known or understood today, there is a revelation of God in the Zodiac, and *that same revelation has been incorporated in the Great Pyramid,[5] and most especially in the Bible*, the inspired Word of God.

But the story which the Bible tells, and the Pyramid also, was written in the stars aeons before either had come into existence. And that is why the psalmist says, " The heavens declare the glory of God; and the firmament sheweth His handywork. Day unto day uttereth speech, and night unto night sheweth knowledge. THERE IS NO SPEECH NOR LANGUAGE, WHERE THEIR VOICE IS NOT HEARD. *Their line is gone out through all the earth, and their words to the end of the world.* In them hath He set a tabernacle for the sun, which is as a bridegroom coming out of his chamber, and rejoiceth as a strong man to run a race. His going forth is from the end of the heaven, and his circuit unto the ends of it: and there is nothing hid from the heat thereof ".[6]

It is to this witness and revelation of the stars that Paul alludes. " But they have not all obeyed the gospel. For Esaias saith, Lord, who hath believed our report? So then faith cometh by hearing, and hearing by the word of God. But I say, HAVE THEY NOT HEARD? Yes verily, *their sound went into all the earth, and their words unto the ends of the world* ".[7]

It is not surprising to learn that, according to Josephus, the signs of the Zodiac were emblazoned on the standards of the twelve tribes of Israel, and these same Zodiacal signs were incorporated in the floor of the Chapel of St. Mary at Glastonbury!

And so this wonderful Glastonbury Zodiac laid out over a vast tract of land ten miles across also witnesses, not to the return of King Arthur the Sun King, but to THE RETURN OF THE LORD JESUS CHRIST,[8] and the Quest for the Holy Graal tells us not of a legendary chalice but of ETERNAL LIFE IN CHRIST JESUS[9] who one day soon will come again to set up His Kingdom and to RULE this earth.[10]

I began by writing of a WELL and a MOUNTAIN, *Chalice Well* and *Glastonbury Tor*. Let me conclude this Chapter with another Mountain and another Well.

The Bible says, " And it shall come to pass in the last days, that the MOUNTAIN of the LORD's house shall be established in the top of the mountains, and shall be exalted above the hills; and *all nations* shall flow unto it. And many people shall go and say, Come ye, and let us go up to the MOUNTAIN OF THE LORD, to the house of the God of Jacob; and He will teach us of His ways, and we will walk in His paths: for out of Zion shall go forth the law, and the word of the LORD from Jerusalem. And He shall judge among the nations, and shall rebuke many people: and they shall beat their swords into plowshares, and their spears into pruninghooks: nation shall not lift up sword against nation, neither shall they learn war any more ".[11]

" And in that day thou shalt say, O LORD, I will praise Thee: though Thou wast angry with me, Thine anger is turned away, and Thou comfortedst me. Behold, God is my salvation; I will trust, and not be afraid: for the LORD JEHOVAH is my strength and my song; He also is become my salvation. Therefore with joy shall ye draw water out of the WELLS OF SALVATION. And in that day shall ye say, Praise the LORD, call upon His name, declare His doings among the people, make mention that His name is exalted. Sing unto the LORD; for He hath done excellent things: this is known in all the earth. Cry out and shout, thou inhabitant of Zion: for great is the Holy One of Israel in the midst of thee ".[12]

Jesus said, " If any man thirst, let him come unto Me, and drink. He that believeth on Me, as the scripture hath said, out of his belly shall flow RIVERS OF LIVING WATER ".[13]

" I am Alpha and Omega, the beginning and the end. I will give unto him that is athirst of the fountain of the WATER OF LIFE freely ".[14]

" And the Spirit and the bride say, Come. And let him that heareth say, Come. And let him that is athirst come. And *whosoever will*, let him take the WATER OF LIFE freely ".[15]

May you TODAY know the reality of those RIVERS of living water!

[1] Numbers 22: 41	[6] Psalm 19: 1-6	[11] Isaiah 2: 2-4
[2] Matthew 26: 27	[7] Romans 10: 16-18	[12] Isaiah 12: 1-6
[3] Isaiah 47: 13	[8] Acts 1: 11	[13] John 7: 37-38
[4] Job 38: 31-32	[9] 1 John 5: 11-12	[14] Revelation 21: 6
[5] Isaiah 19: 19-20	[10] Luke 1: 32-33	[15] Revelation 22: 17

CHAPTER FIVE

ST. PAUL IN BRITAIN

THERE was no greater enemy of the infant Church than Saul of Tarsus. When, shortly after Pentecost, Stephen had been stoned to death by the Jews to become the first Christian martyr, " the witnesses laid down their clothes at a young man's feet, whose name was Saul . . . and Saul was consenting unto his death ".[1] Consumed by religious zeal and impelled by the same spirit of which Jesus spoke, " yea, the time cometh, that whosoever killeth you will think that he doeth God service ",[2] Saul " made havock of the church, entering into every house, and haling men and women committed them to prison ".[3]

As he was later to testify, Saul was " a Jew, born in Tarsus, a city in Cilicia, yet brought up in this city [Jerusalem] at the feet of Gamaliel, and taught according to the perfect manner of the law of the fathers, and was zealous toward God . . . and I persecuted this way unto the death, binding and delivering into prisons both men and women ".[4]

The day came when Saul of Tarsus would go up to Damascus to extend the field of his activities yet further. " And Saul, yet breathing out threatenings and slaughter against the disciples of the Lord, went unto the high priest, and desired of him letters to Damascus to the synagogues, that if he found any of this [Christian] way, whether they were men or women, he might bring them bound unto Jerusalem ".[5] So much for Saul's plan, but God had other plans in mind!

" And as he journeyed, he came near Damascus: and suddenly there shined round about him A LIGHT FROM HEAVEN: and he *fell to the earth,* and heard a VOICE saying unto him, Saul, Saul, why persecutest thou Me? And he said, Who art Thou, Lord? And the Lord said, I AM JESUS WHOM THOU PERSECUTEST: it is hard for thee to kick against the

36

STATUE OF BOADICEA ON THE THAMES EMBANKMENT

Boadicea, more correctly known as Boudicca, exemplifies the spirit of Christian Britannia defying the powers of evil. In A.D. 60 this famous Queen of the Iceni led a revolt of the British tribes against the Roman invaders. Nothing and no one connected with the hated Roman power was spared. Camulodunum (Colchester) and its temple were destroyed, so too were Londinium (London) and Verulamium (St. Albans); *see pages 47-48.*

THE TRIBES OF BRITAIN AT THE TIME OF CHRIST

The Catuvellauni were the most powerful of the British tribes. For fear of them the Trinovantes and other neighbouring tribes became allies of Rome. Thus the objective of the Roman invasion of A.D. 43 was the defeat of the Catuvellauni, the subjugation of the Durotriges and Belgae of the South-west, and the granting of independence to the Iceni and a section of the Atrebates. The Silures played a great part in resisting the conquest, but their leader, Caratacus, was betrayed by Cartimandua, who was Queen of the Brigantes, a client kingdom in the North. In A.D. 60 the Iceni and Trinovantes revolted under Boadicea. Camulodunum (Colchester) and its temple which were intended to mark the permanence of Roman rule in Britain, were destroyed; so too were London and St. Albans.

pricks. And he trembling and astonished said, Lord, what wilt Thou have me to do? And the Lord said unto him, Arise, and go into the city, and it shall be told thee what thou must do. And the men which journeyed with him stood speechless, hearing a voice, but seeing no man. And Saul arose from the earth; and when his eyes were opened, he saw no man: but they led him by the hand, and brought him into Damascus. And he was *three days without sight,* and neither did eat nor drink ".[6]

" And there was a certain disciple at Damascus, named Ananias; and to him said the Lord in a vision, Ananias. And he said, Behold, I am here, Lord. And the Lord said unto him, Arise, and go into *the street which is called Straight,* and inquire in *the house of Judas* for one called *Saul, of Tarsus* "—notice that the Lord has given Ananias the exact name and address!—" for, behold, he prayeth, and hath seen in a vision a man named Ananias coming in, and putting his hand on him, that he might receive his sight ".[7]

" Then Ananias answered, Lord, I have heard by many of this man, how much evil he hath done to Thy saints at Jerusalem: and here he hath authority from the chief priests to bind all that call on Thy name. But the Lord said unto him, Go thy way: for he is *a chosen vessel unto Me,* to bear My name before the GENTILES, and KINGS, and the CHILDREN OF ISRAEL: for I will shew him how great things he must suffer for My name's sake ".[8]

" And Ananias went his way, and entered into the house; and putting his hands on him said, Brother Saul, the Lord, even Jesus, that appeared unto thee in the way as thou camest, hath sent me, that thou mightest receive thy sight, and be filled with the Holy Ghost. And immediately there fell from his eyes as it had been scales: and he received sight forthwith, and arose, and was baptized. And when he had received meat, he was strengthened. Then was Saul certain days with the disciples which were at Damascus. And straightway he preached Christ in the synagogues, that He is the Son of God ".[9]

There we have the conversion of Saul of Tarsus, the arch-persecutor of the Church of God, who became Paul, the great Apostle of the Lord Jesus Christ. What a WONDERFUL story this is! Be sure to read it again from the Bible, and also read the story in Paul's own words as he told it before the Jews at Jerusalem[10] and before King Agrippa at Caesarea. May we say this. JESUS CHRIST IS ALIVE. His power is REAL. He still has power to change men's lives, as He changed this writer's life sixteen years ago. If you ever see Jesus, your life will be changed. If you ever meet the Lord, you will never be the same again!

Now we read in the Bible of the missionary journeys of Paul to Ephesus, Philippi, Corinth, Thessalonica, Colosse, Cyprus, Athens and Malta and the Acts of the Apostles leaves him in Rome. Paul is always thought of as the ' Apostle to the Gentiles ', but how many people have noticed the commission he received of the Lord at the commencement of his ministry? Notice what the Lord told Ananias, " Go thy way: for he [Paul] is *a chosen vessel unto Me,* to bear My name before the GENTILES, and KINGS, and the CHILDREN OF ISRAEL ".[11]

Now we know how Paul fulfilled his commission to the *Gentiles.* Paul himself said, " For He that wrought effectually in Peter to the apostleship of the circumcision [Jews], the same was mighty in me toward the GENTILES ".[12] He spoke also of " the grace that is given to me of God, that I should be the minister of Jesus Christ to the GENTILES . . . to make the GENTILES obedient, by word and deed, through mighty signs and wonders, by the power of the Spirit of God ".[13]

We can see, too, how Paul was used of God to bear Christ's name before *kings.* We read of his appearance before Felix[14], Festus[15] and King Agrippa.[16] We know that the Lord assured him, " Fear not, Paul; thou must be brought before Caesar ".[17]

But when did Paul minister to the CHILDREN OF ISRAEL? We know that Paul did preach to the *Jews,* but as we saw in Chapter One, when Jesus sent His apostles " to the LOST SHEEP OF THE HOUSE OF ISRAEL ",[18] they understood that their ministry was not confined to the Jews in Palestine, but would take them " unto the UTTERMOST PART OF THE EARTH ".[19] *And Paul received exactly the same commission.* He was to bear Christ's name before the CHILDREN OF ISRAEL. Moreover, lest there be any confusion in our minds as to whether it was the Jews who were thus designated, Paul himself tells us that it was Peter who was specifically the apostle of the circumcision [Jews][20] and he, Paul, " strived to preach the gospel, not where Christ was named, lest I should build upon another man's foundation ".[21] So, if Paul was specially commissioned to preach to the CHILDREN OF ISRAEL who were *not the Jews,* how and when did he do so, *and why does the Bible have nothing to say about it?*

Notice how The Acts of the Apostles ends and bear in mind that this is the only *inspired* history we have of the early Church. " And Paul dwelt two whole years in his own hired house, and received all that came in unto him, preaching the kingdom of God, and teaching those things which concern the Lord Jesus Christ, with all confidence, no man forbidding him ".[22] There the record ends. Nothing more is said. There is not so much as an 'Amen' to conclude the record. We find Paul still preaching the gospel of the Kingdom, the same Kingdom about which Jesus taught His apostles and concerning which "they asked of Him, saying, Lord, wilt Thou at this time restore again the kingdom to Israel?", the same Kingdom of God which Jesus said would be "taken from [the Jews], and given to a nation bringing forth the fruits thereof"—we find Paul *still preaching the same message*, and then the Bible record ends abruptly, almost as though the writer had been cut short lest he give vital information away.

Now there are only three books in the New Testament which end without an 'Amen'. They are, as we have just seen, the *Acts of the Apostles*, the General Epistle of *James*, and the *Third Epistle of John*. (Check this fact for yourself—don't just accept our word for it!) This is significant, for we know that " holy men of God spake as they were moved by the Holy Ghost ",[23] and " All scripture is given by inspiration of God ",[24] and so even what the Bible leaves unsaid is of the greatest importance.

The reason that these three books lack an ' Amen ' is that we might understand that they are incomplete. That is to say, they are incomplete not in the sense that anything relevant to personal salvation is concerned, but that they contain *unspoken* information which is not immediately apparent but which, if we are willing for the Holy Spirit to teach us, God Himself will bring to our understanding. In other words, where a book of the New Testament ends without an ' Amen ', the Lord intends us to search its pages to seek out the hidden information which He has reserved for those who will diligently study His Word.

Thus in 3 John we hear of " Diotrephes, who loveth to have the preeminence among them, [and] receiveth us not . . . prating against us with malicious words: and not content therewith, neither doth he himself receive the brethren, and forbiddeth them that would, and casteth them out of the church ".[25] Here, if we will permit the Holy Spirit to open God's Word unto us, is evidence of " the mystery of iniquity ", which, Paul said, " doth already work ".[26] We remember how Paul warned the elders at Ephesus, " Take heed therefore unto yourselves, and to all the flock, over the which the Holy Ghost hath made you overseers, to feed the Church of God, which He hath purchased with His own blood. For I know this, that after my departing shall grievous wolves enter in among you, not sparing the flock. Also of your own selves shall men arise, speaking perverse things, to draw away disciples after them. Therefore watch, and remember, that by the space of three years I ceased not to warn every one night and day with tears ".[27]

So this third epistle of John, short as it is, contains most vital information which it is essential for us to have if we are to understand the apparent division of the supposed Church of God, and the multitudinous sects which we have today. In fact, the historical protestant denominations have their origin, so far as organisation and doctrine are concerned, in the Church of Rome, the counterfeit church so clearly revealed in the Bible and which had begun to be evident in the apostle John's day. (We would, however, except from this statement the Church of England, see page 53.)

Similarly, James gives us hidden information in his epistle which significantly is addressed " to the TWELVE TRIBES which are scattered abroad ".[28] Later he asks, " From whence come wars and fightings among you? ".[29] If we are to take these words literally (and there is no reason why we should not), we infer that, wherever the tribes of Israel were, there was war there. The astonishing fact is that at the time when James wrote his epistle, about A.D. 60, there was warfare only in Parthia and *Britain!*

We do not suggest that this fact *alone* is conclusive evidence of the re-appearance of the tribes of Israel in Britain but it is at least significant. What is important to note is that James does not state the exact location of the twelve tribes. If he had done so, the world would have known the identity of God's Israel people, but His chosen race,[30] His servant nation,[31] had to be hidden from view, themselves completely unaware of their destiny, until such time as the veil should be taken away from their eyes, a day which is fast approaching as Britain learns the hard way that her present humiliation before the world is the result of her abandonment of her sacred trust from God.

To return to the Acts of the Apostles. We have noted that far from telling us the acts of the Twelve Apostles, the book has very little to say about them. They very early vanish from the narrative and, as we have already seen, there is much evidence to prove that some, at least, of the Apostles came to Britain.

Now we suggest that since there is no ' Amen ' at the close of the book of Acts, there must be internal evidence within that book of an important development in the history of the primitive Church, and we suggest that it has to do with Paul's apparently unfulfilled commission to preach the gospel to the children of Israel. As was the case with the Twelve Apostles, and as was the case with " the twelve tribes scattered abroad " mentioned by James, so, we suggest, is the case with Paul. If we knew *where* the Twelve Apostles went, and if we knew *where* Paul eventually got to, we should know where GOD'S ISRAEL PEOPLE WERE. That information had to be restricted that the purposes of God be not frustrated, but now it can be revealed. Notice what the Lord told Daniel, " But thou, O Daniel, shut up the words, and seal the book, even to the TIME OF THE END:, many shall run to and fro, and knowledge shall be increased [and] THE WISE SHALL UNDERSTAND ".[32]

So, *what happened to Paul?* The Acts of the Apostles ends like this, " And Paul dwelt two whole years in his own hired house, and received all that came in unto him, preaching the kingdom of God, and teaching those things which concern the Lord Jesus Christ, with all confidence, no man forbidding him ".[33] It is widely believed that Paul was afterwards set free and that it was at a much later date that he suffered martyrdom in the city of Rome. Meanwhile, *six years of his life are unaccounted for.*

We do know that Paul was intending to visit Spain, for he wrote to the Christians at Rome, " Whensoever I take my journey into Spain, I will come to you: for I trust to see you in my journey . . . When therefore I have performed this . . . I will come by you into Spain ".[34] Did Paul visit Spain, and *did he visit the British Isles?*

Now there is in existence a document known as the 29th Chapter of the Acts of the Apostles. Personally, we do not for one moment believe this to have been written by Luke, nor do we accept it as bearing the marks of divine inspiration. The present writer does not believe that anything needs to be added to the canon of Scripture as we have it, nor yet anything taken away from it. The Bible says, " If any man shall add unto these things, God shall add unto him the plagues that are written in this book: and if any man shall take away from the words of the book of this prophecy, God shall take away his part out of the book of life ".[35]

This document is interesting, however, inasmuch as it purports to describe *a visit of the apostle Paul to Britain.* The document, called the *Sonnini Manuscript,* is supposedly the translation of an original Greek manuscript said to have been found in the archives of Constantinople. There is some question as to the authenticity of this document, but whoever its writer was, he was at least familiar with the tradition that Paul came to London. We reprint it here together with the concluding verses of Acts just as they read in the Bible.

24 And some believed the things which were spoken, and some believed not.
25 And when they agreed not among themselves, they departed, after that Paul had spoken one word, Well spake the Holy Ghost by Esaias the prophet unto our fathers.
26 Saying, Go unto this people, and say, Hearing ye shall hear, and shall not understand; and seeing ye shall see, and not perceive:
27 For the heart of this people is

waxèd gross, and their ears are dull of hearing, and their eyes have they closed; lest they should see with their eyes, and hear with their ears, and understand with their hearts, and should be converted, and I should heal them.

28 Be it known therefore unto you, that the salvation of God is sent unto the Gentiles, and that they will hear it.

29 And when he had said these words, the Jews departed, and had great reasoning among themselves.

30 And Paul dwelt two whole years in his own hired house, and received all that came in unto him.

31 Preaching the kingdom of God, and teaching those things which concern the Lord Jesus Christ, with all confidence, no man forbidding him.

CHAPTER 29

1 And Paul, full of the blessings of Christ, and abounding in the Spirit, departed out of Rome, determining to go into Spain, for he had a long time purposed to journey thitherward, and was minded also to go from thence into Britain.

2 For he had heard in Phoenicia that certain of the children of Israel, about the time of the Assyrian captivity, had escaped by sea to the isles afar off, as spoken by the prophet, and called by the Romans Britain.

3 And the Lord commanded the gospel to be preached far hence to the Gentiles, and to the lost sheep of the house of Israel.

4 And no man hindered Paul; for he testified boldly of Jesus before the tribunes and among the people; and he took with him certain of the brethren which abode with him at Rome, and they took shipping at Ostium, and having the winds fair were brought safely into an haven of Spain.

5 And much people were gathered together from the towns and villages and the hill country; for they had heard of the conversion of the apostle, and the many miracles which he had wrought.

6 And Paul preached mightily in Spain, and great multitudes believed and were converted, for they perceived he was an apostle sent from God.

7 And they departed out of Spain, and Paul and his company finding a ship in Armorica sailing unto Britain, they went therein, and passing along the south coast they reached a port called Raphinus.

8 Now when it was noised abroad that the apostle had landed on their coast, great multitudes of the inhabitants met him. and they treated Paul courteously. and he entered in at the east gate of their city, and lodged in the house of an Hebrew and one of his own nation.

9 And on the morrow he came and stood upon Mount Lud; and the people thronged at the gate, and assembled in the Broadway, and he preached Christ unto them, and many believed the word and the testimony of Jesus.

10 And at even the Holy Ghost fell upon Paul, and he prophesied, saying, Behold, in the last days the God of peace shall dwell in the cities, and the inhabitants thereof shall be numbered; and in the seventh numbering of the people, their eyes shall be opened, and the glory of thèir inheritance shine forth before them. And nations shall come up to worship on the Mount that testifieth of the patience and long suffering of a servant of the Lord.

11 And in the latter days new tidings of the gospel shall issue forth out of Jerusalèm, and the hearts of the people shall rejoice, and behold, fountains shall be opened, and there shall be no more plague.

12 In those days there shall be wars and rumours of wars; and a king shall risè up, and his sword shall be for the healing of the nations, and his peace-making shall abide, and the glory of his kingdom a wonder among princes.

13 And it came to pass that certain of the Druids came unto Paul privately, and showed by their rites and ceremoniès they were descended from the Jews which escaped from bondage in the land of Egypt, and the apostle believed these things, and he gave them the kiss of peace.

14 And Paul abode in his lodgings three months, confirming in the faith and preaching Christ continually.

15 And after these things Paul and his brethren departed from Raphinus, and sailed unto Atium in Gaul.

16 And Paul preached in the Roman garrisons and among the people, exhorting all men to repent and confess their sins.

17 And there came to him certain of the Belgæ to enquire of him of the new doctrine, and of the man Jesus; and Paul opened his heart unto them, and told them all things that had befallen him, how be it that Christ Jesus came into the world to save sinners; and they departed, pondering among themselves upon the things which they had heard.

18 And after much preaching and toil Paul and his fellow labourers passed into Helvetia, and came unto Mount Pontius Pilate, where he who condemned the Lord Jesus dashed himself down headlong, and so miserably perished.

19 And immediately a torrent gushed out of the mountain and washed his body broken in pieces into a lake.

20 And Paul stretched forth his hands upon the water, and prayed unto the Lord, saying, O Lord God, give a sign unto all nations that here Pontius Pilate, which condemned thine only-begotten Son, plunged down headlong into the pit.

21 And while Paul was yet speaking, behold there came a great earthquake, and the face of the waters was changed, and the form of the lake like unto the Son of man hanging in an agony upon the cross.

22 And a voice came out of heaven saying, Even Pilate hath escaped the wrath to come, for he washed his hands before the multitude at the blood-shedding of the Lord Jesus.

23 When, therefore, Paul and those that were with him saw the earthquake, and heard the voice of the angel, they glorified God, and were mightily strengthened in the spirit.

24 And they journeyed and came to Mount Julius, where stood two pillars, one on the right hand and one on the left hand, erected by Caesar Augustus.

25 And Paul, filled with the Holy Ghost, stood up between the two pillars, saying, Men and brethren, these stones which ye see this day shall testify of my journey hence; and verily I say, they shall remain until the out-pouring of the Spirit upon all nations, neither shall the way be hindered throughout all generations.

26 And they went forth and came unto Illyricum, intending to go by Macedonia into Asia, and grace was found in all the churches; and they prospered and had peace. Amen.

Certainly the first fourteen verses of this " Long Lost Chapter of the Acts of the Apostles " are most striking. Mount Lud is, of course, the site of St. Paul's Cathedral and has indeed been the place where people from many nations have worshipped the Lord. " The seventh numbering of the people " could refer to the seventh National Census which was taken in 1861 and it is certainly true that from about that time the scriptural identity of the British people began to be understood. (Write for our FREE book *Britain in Prophecy*.)

The tradition that Paul came to Britain is a strong one. He is said to have preached from the summit of Ludgate Hill where St. Paul's Cathedral now stands. The ancient St. Paul's Cross is said to mark the spot where the apostle stood as he preached the gospel. The reputed presence of Paul in London is said to account for his having been made patron saint of that city. Today, his emblem, the sword of martyrdom, is incorporated in the Coat of Arms of the City of London. Why, if Paul was never here?

Quite apart from these centuries-old traditions, we have abundant evidence in ancient writings of Paul's visit to Britain. It is specifically stated that he came here by Theodoret, Bishop of Cyprus, writing about A.D. 435:

" Paul, liberated from his first captivity at Rome, *preached the gospel to the Britons* and others in the West. Our fishermen and publicans not only persuaded the Romans and their tributaries to acknowledge the Crucified and His laws, but *the Britons also and the Cymry* " (*De Civ. Graec. Off., lib. ix*).

In his commentary on 2 Timothy 4: 16, the same writer says, " When Paul was sent by Festus on his appeal to Rome, he travelled, after being acquitted, into Spain, and thence extended his excursions into other countries, and to *the islands surrounded by the sea* ".

Then Clement of Rome (A.D. 30-100) who is mentioned[36] by Paul in his epistle to the Philippians and is said to have been third Bishop of Rome—Linus was first and Anacletus second—also implies that the apostle visited Britain.

" But not to insist upon ancient examples, let us come to those worthies that have been nearest to us; and take the brave examples of our own age. Through zeal and envy, the most faithful and righteous pillars of the church have been persecuted even to the most grievous deaths. Let us set before our eyes the holy Apostles; Peter by unjust envy underwent not one or two, but many sufferings; till at last being martyred, he went to the place of glory that was due unto him. For the same cause did Paul in like manner receive the reward of his patience. Seven times he was in bonds; he preached both in the East and in the West; leaving behind him the glorious report of his faith: and so having taught the whole world righteousness, and for that end travelled even to the utmost bounds of the West; he at last suffered martyrdom by the command of the governors, and departed out of the world, and went unto his holy place, being become a most eminent pattern of patience unto all ages " (*1 Clement 3: 10-15*).

Notice that Clement speaks of Paul having taken the gospel to the *utmost bounds of the West*, clearly implying the British Isles.

There can be no reasonable doubt that Paul visited and preached in Britain. Such is the testimony of Irenaeus (A.D. 125-189), Tertullian (155-222) and Origen (185-254), of Mello in 256, Eusebius in 315 and Athanasius in 353. The records of the Roman, Eastern, Gallic and Spanish Churches all confirm that Paul preached in Britain, and Capellus in his *History of the Apostles* sums it up by saying,

" I scarcely know of one author, from the times of the Fathers downwards, who does not maintain that St. Paul, after his liberation, preached in every country in Western Europe, *Britain included* ".

MODERN DRUIDS ON GLASTONBURY TOR
The lower picture shows (centre) Chalice Hill and (extreme left) Wearyall Hill

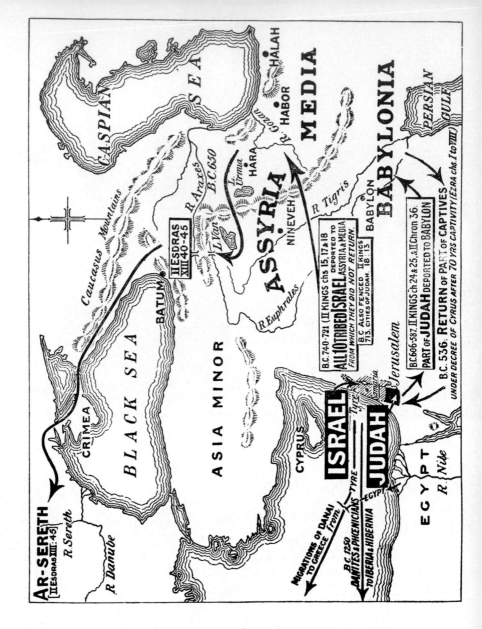

THE MIGRATIONS OF ISRAEL

Note : *Some of the dates shown on the above chart are now found to be incorrect. Ten-tribed Israel was being taken captive by the Assyrians by 735 B.C. The captivity was not complete, however, until 670 B.C., thus fulfilling Isaiah 7: 8. Samaria fell, and the monarchy ended, in 722 B.C. The capivity of Judah began in 604 B.C. and terminated in 534 B.C. after the end of the reign of Darius the Mede in Babylon, thus fulfilling Jeremiah 29: 10.*

We conclude this Chapter with a remarkable report which was published in the *Morning Post,* 27th March, 1931.

"The mayors of Bath, Colchester and Dorchester, and 150 visiting members of the Friends of Italy Society were received today in special audience by the Pope, Pius XI. His Holiness, in a specially prepared address, advanced the theory that it was *St. Paul himself* and not Pope Gregory *who first introduced Christianity* into Britain ".

That a Pope of Rome should in recent times concede that Paul brought the gospel here and that the Church in this land must therefore be of Apostolic and not of Roman origin is remarkable indeed. But we believe that claim to be absolutely TRUE! It is the conclusion that the Bible leads us to, and history confirms it. In the next Chapter we shall show the remarkable circumstances behind Paul's visit to Britain and how the British Royal Family embraced the faith of Christ.

1 Acts 7: 58; 8: 1
2 John 16: 2
3 Acts 8: 3
4 Acts 22: 3-4
5 Acts 9: 1-2
6 Acts 9: 3-9
7 Acts 9: 10-12
8 Acts 9: 13-16
9 Acts 9: 17-20
10 Acts 22: 1-21
11 Acts 9: 15
12 Galatians 2: 8

13 Romans 15: 15-19
14 Acts 24: 1-27
15 Acts 25: 1-27
16 Acts 26: 1-32
17 Acts 27: 24
18 Matthew 10: 6
19 Acts 1: 8
20 Galatians 2: 7-8
21 Romans 15: 20
22 Acts 28: 30-31
23 2 Peter 1: 21
24 2 Timothy 3: 16

25 3 John 9-10
26 2 Thessalonians 2: 7
27 Acts 20: 28-31
28 James 1: 1
29 James 4: 1
30 Deuteronomy 7: 6
31 Isaiah 41: 8
32 Daniel 12: 4, 10
33 Acts 28: 30-31
34 Romans 15: 24-28
35 Revelation 22: 18-19
36 Philippians 4: 3

CHAPTER SIX

THE BRITISH ROYAL FAMILY AT ROME

THE circumstances of Paul's coming to Britain present a most wonderful and dramatic story, and throw light upon an era in early British history about which comparatively little is understood today.

At the time of Christ, the Roman Empire had reached the zenith of its power. It occupied the whole of Europe, Northern Africa and Asia. However, Britain remained undefeated. Julius Caesar had, it is true, carried out a reconnaissance raid in August, 55 B.C., and had stayed two weeks, and had attempted an invasion in July of the following year, this time staying for two months. Five small tribes in Kent had promised submission, hostages had been taken, and the Trinovantes had, out of fear of their neighbours the Catuvellauni, become allies of Rome. But that was all. Britain was left alone for almost a century.

Then in A.D. 43, i.e., ten years after the Crucifixion and only six years after the coming of Joseph of Arimathæa, Claudius the Roman Emperor launched a full-scale invasion of Britain, despatching four legions, the II Augusta, IX Hispana, XIV Gemina and XX Valeria Victrix—some 25,000 men in all—under the command of Aulus Plautius. The map facing page 37 shows the tribes of Britain at about this time.

This was the commencement of a bloody and protracted war in which the might of Rome was completely unable to subdue the stubborn British people. The British forces led by Caradoc, King of the Silures, put up an indomitable resistance for more than seven years. Caradoc, better known as Caratacus, was the son of Bran the Blessed, and grandson of King Lear. He is usually described as the son of Cunobelinus, confusion having arisen out of the fact that following the death of Cunobelinus it was Caratacus who became military leader of the British tribes.

46

Then in A.D. 51, Caratacus was defeated in North Wales and fled to the North where, presumably, he intended to rally the support of the Brigantes. But their Queen, Cartimandua, had entered into a treaty with Rome, Caratacus was handed over, and he and his wife, his daughter Gladys and his father Bran, were taken captive to Rome.

It was the Roman custom to put their defeated enemies to death, but such was the fame and renown of Caradoc that he was received in Rome like a hero and was permitted to speak in his own defence before the Emperor Claudius and assembled Senate. His great oration has been preserved for us in Tacitus' *Annals.*

" Had my government in Britain been directed solely with a view to the preservation of my hereditary domains, or the aggrandisement of my own family, I might long since have entered this city an ally, not a prisoner; nor would you have disdained for a friend a king descended from illustrious ancestors, and the dictator of many nations. My present condition, stript of its former majesty, is as adverse to myself as it is a cause of triumph to you. What then? I was lord of men, horses, arms, wealth: what wonder if at your dictation I refused to resign them? Does it follow, that because the Romans aspire to universal dominion, every nation is to accept the vassalage they would impose? I am now in your power—betrayed, not conquered. Had I, like others, yielded without resistance, where would have been the name of Caradoc? Where your glory? Oblivion would have buried both in the same tomb. Bid me live, I shall survive for ever in history one example at least of Roman clemency ".

So Caradoc and his family were not only spared but were permitted to make their home in Rome, though not being allowed for the time being to return to Britain. We shall return to Caradoc in a moment.

Meanwhile the war in Britain continued unabated. A new offensive was launched in Wales having as its objective the destruction of the Druids' stronghold on Mona (Anglesey). The Druids were fiercely nationalistic, a unifying force amongst the tribes of Britain, and regarded by Rome as a dangerous subversive movement. They were ruthlessly massacred and their groves destroyed.

While the legions were still in North Wales the British tribes revolted. This was in the year A.D. 60 when we hear for the first time of the famous Queen Boudicca, better known (though incorrectly) as Boadicea. Her husband Prasutagus, King of the Iceni, had died leaving his considerable wealth to Nero (who had succeeded Claudius as Emperor) and to his own daughters, evidently intending to secure their protection. However, the Roman procurator Catus Decianus confiscated the estate and began to seize the property of the nobles. Boadicea was flogged and her daughters raped.

The Iceni, hitherto the most submissive of the British tribes, revolted. So did the Trinovantes, their neighbours and former enemies, who had been suffering under the heavy burden of taxation for the maintenance of the Temple at Camulodunum (Colchester) where the Emperor was worshipped. Boadicea found herself at the head of a great army, perhaps 100,000 strong, nearly all the Britons within reach rallying to her support. We are reminded of Deborah who also led an army into battle in Bible days.[1]

Camulodunum was laid waste. So too were Londinium (London) and Verulamium (St. Albans). Nothing and no one connected with the hated Roman power was spared, and recent excavations have disclosed in these cities a layer of ash giving some idea of the extent of the destruction that took place. However, the might and skill of Roman arms eventually triumphed. The British were defeated, and Boadicea, rather than fall into enemy hands, committed suicide.

We feel sure that this brief mention of the illustrious British Queen will be of interest to our readers. There is a magnificent statue of Boadicea on Westminster Bridge, London—see the picture facing page 36—and she exemplifies the spirit of Christian *Britannia*, defying the powers of evil, as portrayed on our coins even today.

But we must return to Caradoc, or as he was now known, Caratacus, living in exile in Rome with his family. His daughter Gladys would have been about seven years of age at the time of their being taken to Rome and we understand that the Emperor Claudius adopted her into his household, giving her the name Claudia. Claudia eventually married a noble Roman senator whose name was Rufus Pudens.

This is especially interesting because Rufus was the friend of the poet Martial in whose *Epigrams* he features. One of them says, " Claudia, the fair one from a foreign shore, is with my Pudens joined in wedlock's band " (*iv, 32*), and another, " Our Claudia, named Ruffina, sprung we know from blue-eyed Britons " (*xi, 40*).

It is, we believe, this Rufus Pudens whom Paul greets in his letter to the Romans where he says, " Salute Rufus chosen in the Lord, and his mother and mine ".[2] This almost suggests that Rufus and Paul might have had *the same mother* (though not the same father), that is to say they could have been *half-brothers*. It is certain that no one could claim to have been Paul's mother in the spiritual sense. As we have already seen (page 37), there was no human agency in Paul's conversion, nor did he have a human teacher.[3]

So now we have the interesting circumstance of the British Royal Family being exiled in Rome, but the astonishing thing is that PAUL WAS AT ROME AT THE SAME TIME! Notice it in your Bible, the last two verses of the Acts of the Apostles, " And Paul dwelt two whole years in his own hired house, and received all that came in unto him, preaching the kingdom of God, and teaching those things which concern the Lord Jesus Christ, with all confidence, no man forbidding him ".[4]

How remarkable this is. As Paul himself remarked on another occasion, " How unsearchable are His judgments, and His ways past finding out! For who hath known the mind of the Lord? or who hath been His counsellor?"[5] Here is Paul, the great apostle, a prisoner in Rome, and here is Caratacus, King of Siluria, also a prisoner in the same city. Paul, with a commission as yet unfulfilled to take the gospel to the children of Israel,[6] and Caratacus, a British King whose life has been miraculously spared waiting in due course to return to Britain!

Here we have the most wonderful illustration of one of the greatest truths of the Christian life. " And we know that ALL THINGS WORK TOGETHER FOR GOOD to them that *love God*, to them who are the *called according to His purpose* ".[7] If it seemed a sad restriction on Paul for him to be imprisoned at Rome, and a tragedy for Caradoc for him to have been betrayed in Britain, yet a purpose was being worked out through it all, the legacy of which remains to this day.

Now we know from the Bible that although a prisoner at Rome, yet Paul enjoyed a measure of freedom. He " dwelt two whole years in his own hired house, and received all that came in unto him ". Similarly, Caradoc and his family lived in the *Palatium Britannicum* or British Palace, now known as St. Pudentiana. In much later years Pudens and his four children, Timotheus, Novatus, Pudentiana and Prassedis, were all to suffer martyrdom; Claudia predeceased them, possibly martyred too.

Now it is surely without question that Caradoc, coming from Britain which had received the gospel only a few years earlier under Joseph of Arimathæa, *would be anxious to hear the gospel from the lips of the great apostle himself.* Would not the renowned British King and the famed apostle have become intimately acquainted? And did not the Lord say of Paul, " He is a chosen vessel unto Me, to bear My name before the Gentiles, and KINGS, and the CHILDREN OF ISRAEL "?[8] Was not Caratacus a KING and were not his people of ISRAEL stock?

Notice the letter Paul wrote from Rome when he sends greetings to Timothy, " Do thy diligence to come before winter. EUBULUS greeteth thee, and PUDENS, and LINUS, and CLAUDIA, and *all the brethren* ".[9] We said in Chapter Two that the Church met in the house (see page 18). The Pudens, Linus and Claudia mentioned here could be no other than the son-in-law, son and daughter of Caratacus, and " all the brethren " other Christians meeting in the same house. Thus, if they were not already converted, *the British Royal Family embraced the faith of Christ while yet at Rome.*

This, we believe, is the background to Paul's visit to Britain. That such a visit was made seems irrefutable: we quoted some of the historical evidence in the last Chapter. Notice again Theodoret's testimony, about A.D. 435:

"Paul, liberated from his first captivity at Rome. *preached the gospel to the Britons* and others in the West. Our fishermen and publicans not only persuaded the Romans and their tributaries to acknowledge the Crucified and His laws, but *the Britons also and the Cy.nry*" (De Civ. Graec. Off., lib. ix).

Then notice what Alford says in his *Regia Fides*:

"It is perfectly certain that before St. Paul had come to Rome Aristobulus was absent in Britain, and it is confessed by all that Claudia was a British lady" (Volume I, page 83).

Who was Aristobulus? He is mentioned by Paul in his Epistle to the Romans, written from Corinth about A.D. 60. Paul says, "Salute Apelles approved in Christ. Salute them which are of *Aristobulus' household*".[10] Clearly Aristobulus was absent from Rome at that time, and the earliest writers indicate that he came to Britain and was martyred here.

Dorotheus, writing about A.D. 303, says:

"Aristobulus, who is mentioned by the Apostle in his Epistle to the Romans, was made bishop in Britain".

Haleca, Bishop of Augusta, says:

"The memory of many martyrs is celebrated by the Britons, especially that of St. Aristobulus, one of the seventy disciples".

The *Martyrologia* of Adonis tells us under 17th March:

"Natal day of Aristobulus, Bishop of Britain, brother of St. Barnabas the Apostle, by whom he was ordained bishop. He was sent to Britain where, after preaching the truth of Christ and forming a Church, he received martyrdom".

The *Martyrologies* of the Greek Churches inform us under 15th March:

"Aristobulus was one of the seventy disciples and a follower of St. Paul the Apostle, along with whom he preached the Gospel to the whole world and ministered to him. He was chosen by St. Paul to be missionary bishop to the land of Britain, inhabited by a very warlike and fierce race. By them he was often scourged and repeatedly dragged as a criminal through their towns, yet he converted many of them to Christianity. He was there martyred after he had built churches and ordained deacons and priests for the island".

Then, according to the *Genealogies of the Saints of Britain,* "These came with Bran the Blessed from Rome to Britain—Arwystli Hen (Senex) [i.e. Aristobulus the Aged], Ilid, Cyndaw, men of Israel; Maw, or Manaw, son of Arwystli Hen".

Thus it was that the apostle Paul came to Britain. The way was opened up through the auspices of the British Royal Family at Rome. Though Caradoc was compelled to remain in Rome until the expiration of his seven years detention, his family were free to return whenever they wished. The Welsh Triads tell us that Bran, the father of Caradoc, after being baptised in Rome, returned to Britain and thereafter fostered the Church in Siluria (South Wales). Bran was accompanied by Aristobulus.

And so twice within the quarter century following the Crucifixion, the gospel was carried to Britain and received Royal patronage. Joseph's mission to Glastonbury was fostered by King Arviragus, and Paul's mission to the Silures was sponsored by Caradoc. And so, in ministering to the people of these islands, the final part of Paul's commission " to bear My name before the Gentiles, and kings, and the *children of Israel*" was fulfilled.

The British Church has always been a royal one. Its first converts were members of the British Royal Family. Its nominal head has always been the reigning Sovereign, and today as head of Church and State, Her Majesty Queen Elizabeth II sits upon the Throne of David[11] established over God's Israel people in these British Isles. How MARVELLOUSLY God's Word has been fulfilled.

" Listen, O ISLES, unto Me . . . Thou art My servant, O ISRAEL, in whom I will be glorified . . . It is a light thing that thou shouldest be My servant to raise up the tribes of Jacob, and to restore the preserved of Israel: I will also give thee for a light to the Gentiles, that thou mayest be My salvation unto THE END OF THE EARTH ".[12] " KINGS shall see and arise, PRINCES also shall worship . . . Behold, these shall come from far: and, lo, these from the NORTH and from the WEST ".[13] " And KINGS shall be thy *nursing fathers*, and their QUEENS thy *nursing mothers* ".[14]

" Arise, shine; for thy light is come, and the glory of the LORD is risen upon thee . . . and the Gentiles shall come to thy light, and KINGS to the brightness of thy rising . . . Thy sons shall come from far, and thy daughters shall be nursed at thy side ".[15] " And the sons of strangers shall build up thy walls, and their KINGS shall minister unto thee ".[16] " Thou shalt also suck the milk of the Gentiles, and shalt *suck the breast of KINGS* ".[17]

" And I will set a sign among them, and I will send those that escape of them unto the nations . . . to the ISLES AFAR OFF . . . and they shall declare My glory among the Gentiles ".[18] " Thy people also shall be all righteous: they shall inherit the land for ever, the branch of My planting, the work of My hands, that I may be glorified. A little one shall become a thousand, and a small one a strong nation: I the LORD will hasten it in his time ".[19]

[1] Judges 4: 4-24
[2] Romans 16: 13
[3] Galatians 1: 11-12
[4] Acts 28: 30-31
[5] Romans 11: 33-34
[6] Acts 9: 15
[7] Romans 8: 28
[8] Acts 9: 15
[9] 2 Timothy 4: 21
[10] Romans 16: 10
[11] Jeremiah 33: 17
[12] Isaiah 49: 1-6
[13] Isaiah 49: 7-12
[14] Isaiah 49: 23
[15] Isaiah 60: 1-4
[16] Isaiah 60: 10
[17] Isaiah 60: 16
[18] Isaiah 66: 19
[19] Isaiah 60: 21-22

CHAPTER SEVEN

THE EARLY CHURCH IN BRITAIN

PERHAPS this is a good point to sum up what we have learned so far. We have shown that the Twelve Apostles were commissioned to preach the gospel of the Kingdom[1] to the lost sheep of the house of Israel,[2] and we have seen that their commission took them " unto the uttermost part of the earth ",[3] to the British Isles. We have seen that Paul himself with a similar commission " to bear [Christ's] name before the Gentiles, and kings, and the children of Israel ",[4] also came " to the utmost bounds of the West ".[5] We have shown that even before these arrived in Britain, Joseph of Arimathæa had been sent here by the Apostle Philip, and that twice within the first quarter century after the Resurrection the faith of Christ had received Royal patronage in these islands. We have shown also that while there was a true company of God's people in Rome to whom Paul wrote,[6] there was also in that city a counterfeit church which has come down to us today as the Roman Catholic Church.

Some years ago the B.B.C. in a schools' broadcast stated that St. Augustine was the first person to introduce Christianity to Britain in A.D. 597. Augustine was sent to Britain by Pope Gregory I, and so it has become a matter of general belief that Britain was always Roman Catholic until the time of the Reformation. However, nothing could be further from the truth.

Britain was the first of all peoples *nationally* to embrace the faith of the Lord Jesus Christ. The *national* conversion of Britain to Christianity may perhaps be attributed to King Lucius (see page 30). We do not suggest that the *pure* faith was widely maintained in the centuries that followed. Jesus said, " Fear not, *little flock*; for it is your Father's good pleasure to give you the kingdom ",[7] and Paul warned that " after my departing shall

CELTIC CROSS DISCOVERED AT GLASTONBURY

Dr. C. A. Rulegh Radford and Mr. Philip Rahtz examine the stone cross which was found during excavations on Glastonbury Tor, September, 1966

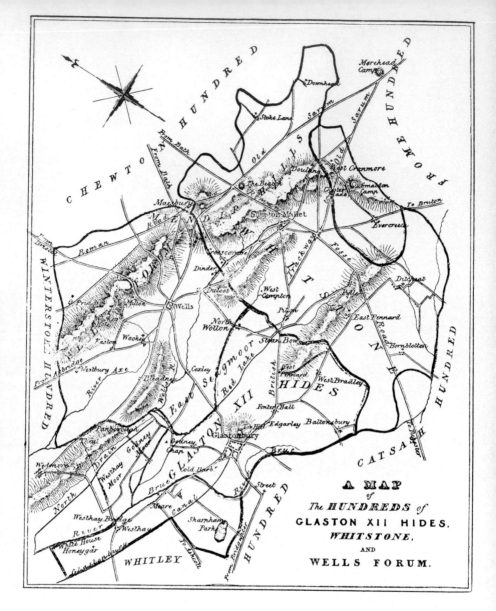

MAP OF GLASTON XII HIDES

The twelve hides of Glastonbury are mentioned in Domesday Book, 1087, as never having paid tax. The land is said to have been given to Joseph of Arimathæa and his companions by King Arviragus immediately after their arrival in Britain, see page 19.

grievous wolves enter in among you, not sparing the flock ".[8] It has always been the remnant within the ' Church ' which has sought to " earnestly contend for the faith which was once delivered unto the saints ".[9] Nevertheless, Britain had become a Christian nation long before Augustine reached these shores, and in fact, long before there was a ' pope ' in Rome. (The bishops of Rome were never styled ' popes ' until the sixth century).

When Augustine landed on these shores he was met by bishops of the British Church who told him:

" Be it known and declared that we all, individually and collectively, are in all humility prepared to defer to the Church of God, and to the Bishop of Rome, and to every sincere and godly Christian, so far as to love every one according to his degree, in perfect charity, and to assist them all by word and in deed in becoming the children of God. But as for any other obedience, we know of none that he, whom you term Pope, or Bishop of Bishops, can demand. The deference we have mentioned we are ready to pay to him as to every other Christian, but in all other respects our obedience is due to the jurisdiction of the Bishop of Caerleon, who is alone under God our ruler to keep us right in the way of salvation " *(Spelman, Concilia, pp. 108-9).*

We may well ask, if Augustine introduced Christianity to these islands, who were these bishops by whom he was met? The fact is, the gospel had been preached in this land for five-and-a-half centuries already. There was a flourishing Church in Britain; indeed hundreds if not thousands of British Christians were martyred during the Diocletian persecution when the Roman Emperor determined to exterminate Christianity. Today, the City of St. Albans is named after the best-known martyr of that period. Gildas (516-570), the noted historian, tells us:

" There were martyred in Britain, Stephen and Argulius, both Bishops of London; Socrates, Bishop of York; Amphibalus, Bishop of Llandaff; Nicholas, Bishop of Penrhyn; Melior, Bishop of Carlisle; St. Alban; Julius and Aaron, priests of Caerleon; and 889 communicants in different grades of society " *(De Excidio Britanniae, Sec. 10, p. 10).*

So there was a British Church at that time, but it was not Roman Catholic! The word ' catholic ' means simply *universal.* The Church in this land was ' catholic ' inasmuch as it embraced the *universal* faith of the gospel. That faith has its origin in the New Testament Scriptures and not in Rome. The Church in Britain could also claim to be ' apostolic ', i.e. it was founded by the original Apostles of the Lord Jesus Christ. It can, in fact lay far more claim to being truly apostolic than can the Roman Catholic Church which, as we explained on page 12, was not founded by Peter but by an imposter masquerading as the apostle of Christ.

Then today the Church of England is also described as ' protestant,' i.e. it is opposed to the claims of the Pope and protests against them. However, protestantism is no mere negative belief but a positive assertion that the Scriptures contain all that is requisite for salvation, that " by grace are ye saved through faith; and that not of yourselves: it is the gift of God: not of works, lest any man should boast ".[10] Unhappily, we are living in days of deepening apostasy so that many of these distinctions have been deliberately ignored, and the very truths for which men gave their lives are being compromised and treated with contempt.

We mentioned the Diocletian persecution in which so many died, but the Church has always thrived in persecution: the blood of the martyrs has ever been the seed of the Church. Within ten years the British Church was sufficiently flourishing as to send three bishops, Eborius of York, Restitutus of London, and Adelfius of Caerleon, to the Council of Arles, convened in A.D. 314 by the Emperor Constantine. British bishops were also present at the Council of Nicæa in 325 (when the Nicene Creed was formulated), at the Council of Sardica in 347, and the Council of Ariminium in 359.

Now notice the testimony of the greatest Church historians of early days.

Tertullian (155-222) informs us:

"The extremities of Spain, the various parts of Gaul, the regions of Britain which have never been penetrated by Roman arms have received the religion of Christ " (*Tertullian Def. Fidei, p. 179*).

Eusebius (265-340), the Church's first great historian, says:

"The Apostles passed beyond the ocean to the isles called the Britannic Isles " (*De Demonstratione Evangelii. Lib. III*).

Chrysostom (347-407), who was the Patriarch of Constantinople, tells us:

"Though thou shouldest go to the ocean to the British Isles, there thou shouldest hear all men everywhere discoursing matters out of the Scriptures with another voice, but not another faith, with a different tongue but the same judgment " (*Chrysostomi Orat. O Theos Xristos*).

Gildas (516-570), whom we have already quoted, writes:

"Christ, the True Sun, afforded His light, the knowledge of His precepts, to our island during the height of [or, the last year of] the reign of Tiberius Caesar " (*De Excidio Britanniae, Sec. 8, p. 25*).

Tiberius Caesar died in A.D. 37, and, as we have shown in Chapter Two, it was in this year that Joseph of Arimathæa came to Britain:

Theodoret, writing in A.D. 435 says:

"Paul, liberated from his first captivity at Rome, preached the Gospel to the Britons and others in the West. Our fishermen and publicans not only persuaded the Romans and their tributaries to acknowledge the Crucified and His laws, but the Britons also and the Cymry " (*De Civ. Graec. Off., lib. ix*).

Bede (670-735) in his *Ecclesiastical History of the English Nation*, tells us:

"The Britons preserved the faith which they had received, uncorrupted and entire, in peace and tranquility until the time of the Emperor Diocletian" (*J. M. Dent Everyman's Edn., p. 9*).

Bede was, of course, a Roman Catholic, and he has given us a most telling account of the faith of the Church in Britain at the coming of Augustine:

"For they did not keep Easter Sunday at the proper time, but from the fourteenth to the twentieth moon; which computation is contained in a revolution of eighty-four years. Besides, they did several other things which were against the unity of the Church . . . After a long disputation, they did not comply with the entreaties, exhortations, or rebukes of Augustine and his companions, but preferred their own traditions before all the churches in the world . . . They could not depart from their ancient customs without the consent and leave of their people" (*J. M. Dent, Everyman's Edn., pp. 65-66*).

This testimony is most important since it shows us once again that the Church had been in existence in Britain long before the coming of Augustine in 597, and also because it reveals the British Churches' refusal to accept the rule of Rome. The Church of this nation would from its earliest days have observed the Passover on the fourteenth day of the month, in common with the Eastern Church. The Roman Catholic 'Easter' which was later introduced had its origin in paganism.

Thus the evidence is irrefutable. *The Church in Britain antedates the coming of Augustine by more than five-and-a-half centuries.* Moreover, it is only in comparatively recent times that the great antiquity of the British Church seems to have been lost sight of. The primacy of the Church in Britain was taken for granted until the matter was raised by ambassadors of France and Spain in 1409, and then at four successive Church Councils, Pisa 1409, Constance 1417, Sienna 1424 and Basle 1434, the French and Spanish churches conceded that they must yield precedence to the British.

Archbishop Ussher (1581-1656) informs us that the basis of the British claim was the burial of Joseph of Arimathæa at Glastonbury, and the donation by Arviragus of the twelve hides of land. Ussher, who is best remembered for his system of Bible Chronology incorporated in the margin of many Bibles even today, tells us:

"The Mother Church of the British Isles is the Church in Insula Avalonia, called by the Saxons 'Glaston'".

Robert Parsons, the Jesuit, states in his *Three Conversions of England* :

"Christian religion began in Britain within fifty years of Christ's Ascension".

Polydore Virgil (1470-1555), Archbishop of Wells, who was from a literary family, was steeped in English history, and had special access to sources of the Glastonbury tradition, tells us:

" Britain, partly through Joseph of Arimathæa, partly through Fugatus and Damianus [Fagan and Dyfan], was of all kingdoms the first that received the Gospel ".

Sir Henry Spelman in his *Concilia*, wrote:

" It is certain that Britain received the faith in the first age from the first sowers of the Word. Of all the churches whose origin I have investigated in Britain, the Church of Glastonbury is the most ancient . . . we have abundant evidence that this Britain of ours received the faith and that from the disciples of Christ Himself, soon after the Crucifixion of Christ ".

Cardinal Pole said:

" The See Apostolic [Rome] from whence I come hath a special respect to this realm above all others, and not without cause, seeing that God Himself, as it were, by providence hath given to this realm prerogative of nobility above all others, which to make plain unto you, it is to be considered that this island first of all islands received the light of Christ's religion ".

The occasion of this speech was the Assembly of the Lords and Commons before Philip and Mary in Whitehall for the Act of Reconciliation, the acceptance by the British Church of the Pope of Rome. In a speech made the following day at Westminster Abbey, Cardinal Pole said:

" Once again God hath given a token of His special favour to the Realm, for as this nation in the time of the primitive Church was the first to be called out of the darkness of heathenism, so now they are the first to whom God has given grace to repent of their schism ".

Having then established the fact that the Church in Britain can lay claim to apostolic foundation[11] and does not owe its origin to Augustine, it will be profitable for us to say a few words about the native Church in the earliest centuries.

During the first three centuries of the Christian era there were bands of Christians in various parts of Ireland. However, it is to Patrick that the conversion of Ireland is usually attributed. The centuries have obliterated every clue as to the birthplace of Patrick but it seems likely that he was born in Western Britain, a Roman citizen of Christian parentage. The date may have been 385. When he was about 16 years of age he and his family were taken captive to Ireland by raiders who came in from the sea. After seven years he escaped to Britain but later returned as Bishop of Ireland in 432. Patrick now evangelised the whole of Ireland, and from schools founded by him, missionaries took the light of the gospel to every part of Europe. Patrick died on 17th March, 461.

It was from Ireland that Columba passed into Scotland. Columba was born in Ireland on 7th December, 521. He was of royal parentage, his father being a member of the reigning house in Ireland, descendants of Niall of the Nine Hostages, the king who was reigning in Ireland at the time when Patrick had been brought from Britain as a slave. His mother Eithne belonged to the royal house of Leinster. Thus Columba might well have been King of Ireland had not divine providence decreed otherwise.

In circumstances which need not concern us here, Columba left Ireland in May, 563, and came to Iona, the tiny island off the Atlantic coast of Scotland. From here he converted almost the whole of Scotland, and missionaries were sent forth into the north of England and much of Europe. The number of churches which Columba founded in Scotland alone is variously estimated at from 53 to more than 300. He died in 597, the very same year that Augustine arrived in Britain.

Here we should explain that during the fifth and sixth centuries, Britain had been invaded by pagan Jutes, Saxons and Angles—all Israelite people nonetheless—with the result that the native British Church had been driven into the West and North. It was now the Celtic Church, the legacy of such as Patrick and Columba, which was destined to rekindle the light of Christ, and not the Augustinian mission which met with little success outside of Kent.

Oswald, King of Northumbria had become a Christian during a period of exile on the island of Iona. Aidan was now sent from Iona to aid Oswald in the conversion of his people, and established himself on the island of Lindisfarne which now became a wellspring of Christianity in the North. Aidan has been called the apostle of the English.

Thus it was the Celtic Church which was responsible for the evangelisation of these islands, becoming the lantern of the West, and sending forth missionaries all over Europe. During the seventh century Iona was at the height of its fame.

It was during this century however, that Roman influence, first introduced by Augustine (who had died in 604) began to make itself felt. As we have seen from the statements of Bede already quoted, there was marked resentment on the part of the British Church to the encroachment of Rome. In 664, a Synod was convoked at Whitby, presided over by Oswy, King of Northumbria, for the purpose of settling the date of Easter. This ended with the defeat and resignation of Colman, Bishop of Northumbria. Roman usage was accepted on three points, and the Church now moved towards Rome, thus paving the way for that complete domination which lasted until the middle of the sixteenth century.

The native Church, both British and Celtic, which until this time had been distinguished for its piety and evangelistic zeal, now began to acquire centralised control, and a unified system of Church Government was established under Theodore of Tarsus who became the first Archbishop of Canterbury in 667. But this usurpation by Rome was long resented, and four centuries later we find William, the Norman Conqueror of England, refusing to acknowledge the claims of the Pope, " Fealty I have never willed to do, nor will I do it now. I have never promised it, nor do I find that my predecessors did it to yours ".

We have told but a little of the wonderful story of the early Church in Britain. From its earliest days it has been bound up with the origin, the growth and the development of the nation. The rival kingdoms existing in these Isles at the time of Christ— see the map facing page 37—were brought into spiritual and national unity. The pagan Jutes, Saxons and Angles became peace-loving and civilised. And in the centuries which followed, it was the Church which established schools where children might be taught, and hospitals and almshouses where the sick and aged might be cared for. It covered the land with cathedrals and churches of unexampled beauty. It translated the Scriptures which are able to make men " wise unto salvation through faith which is in Christ Jesus ".[12] It made the Bible an open book, and taught successive generations the knowledge and love of God. Thus it was the Church which became the strongest element in the formation of the national character. The respect for authority, the concept of service, the love of freedom—ideals which were to become Britain's greatest contribution to the world—were fostered by the Church.

But this moulding of the national character, the preparation of the British people for a role in which they were destined to bless the world, could never have taken place unless the faith which was planted here in Bible days had been preserved continuously all down the centuries. This island home of ours can truly claim that its Church was founded by the Apostles, that it recognises the Scriptures as its sole rule of faith and doctrine, and that it is subject to no other Church on earth. Moreover, it has reason to believe that the Saviour of the world Himself *visited the place of its foundation.* This shall be the subject of our next Chapter.

[1] Matthew 4: 23
[2] Matthew 10: 6
[3] Acts 1: 8
[4] Acts 9: 15
[5] 1 Clement 3: 14
[6] Romans 1: 7
[7] Luke 12: 32
[8] Acts 20: 29
[9] Jude 3
[10] Ephesians 2: 8-9
[11] Ephesians 2: 20
[12] 2 Timothy 3: 15

CHAPTER EIGHT

DID JESUS EVER COME TO BRITAIN?

TO suggest that Jesus may once have come to Britain sounds almost too wonderful for words, yet the astonishing fact is that in no less than twenty places in the South-west of England there are firm traditions of Jesus having visited these Islands during the "hidden years" when the Bible is entirely silent concerning His movements. These traditions find their expression in the words of "Jerusalem" written by the poet and mystic William Blake (1757-1827).

> And did Those feet in ancient time
> Walk upon England's mountains green?
> And was the Holy Lamb of God
> On England's pleasant pastures seen?
> And did the Countenance Divine
> Shine forth upon our clouded hills?
> And was Jerusalem builded here
> Among those dark Satanic mills?
>
> Bring me my bow of burning gold!
> Bring me my arrows of desire!
> Bring me my spear! O clouds unfold!
> Bring me my chariot of fire!
> I will not cease from mental fight,
> Nor shall my sword sleep in my hand,
> Till I have built Jerusalem
> In England's green and pleasant land.

This famous hymn has become an integral part of our national life. In 1935, on the occasion of the Jubilee of the late King George V, a great National concert was held in the Royal Albert Hall. At the close, an additional item was sung by request of the King. It was "Jerusalem". Thus the famous hall resounded with the strains of this inspiring hymn which terminates with the prayer that this land shall become even as Jerusalem of which the Lord said, " Then there shall be a place which the LORD your God shall choose to cause His name to dwell there ".[1] Yet how many of the millions who have sung those words, set to Sir Hubert Parry's wonderful music, have paused to think about the words or to consider their meaning?

Evidently, Blake was familiar with the tradition that Jesus came to Britain either as a child or as a young man. That tradition still survives today in parts of Cornwall and Somerset, being especially linked with Glastonbury and places like Priddy and Pilton in the Mendips.

One's first impulse might be to dismiss these traditions as mere fables but we do well to remember that legend is not fiction, nor is truth confined only to that which can be established by documentary evidence. In the absence of positive proof to the contrary—and there is nothing whatever in the Gospels about the eighteen missing years of Jesus' life, only an intimation that He may have been away—there is no reason why one should not accept such traditions as having a foundation in fact. As we showed in Chapter Five, truth may often be adduced from a *lack* of information or even a complete *silence*.

Now the Bible is ENTIRELY SILENT about Jesus' movements between the ages of 12 and 30. The only incident of childhood recorded in the Gospels is His visit to the Temple at the age of twelve.

" Now His parents went to Jerusalem every year at the feast of the Passover. And when He was twelve years old, they went up to Jerusalem after the custom of the feast. And when they had fulfilled the days, as they returned, the child Jesus tarried behind in Jerusalem; and Joseph and His mother knew not of it. But they, supposing Him to have been in the company, went a day's journey; and they sought Him among their kinsfolk and acquaintance. And when they found Him not, they turned back again to Jerusalem, seeking Him. And it came to pass, that after three days they found Him in the temple, sitting in the midst of the doctors, both hearing them, and asking them questions. And all that heard Him were astonished at His understanding and answers. And when they saw Him, they were amazed: and His mother said unto Him, Son, why hast thou thus dealt with us? behold, Thy father and I have sought thee sorrowing. And He said unto them, How is it that ye sought Me? wist ye not that I must be about My Father's business? And they understood not

PILGRIMAGE AT GLASTONBURY

Thousands gather for the Annual Pilgrimage held on the last Saturday in June.

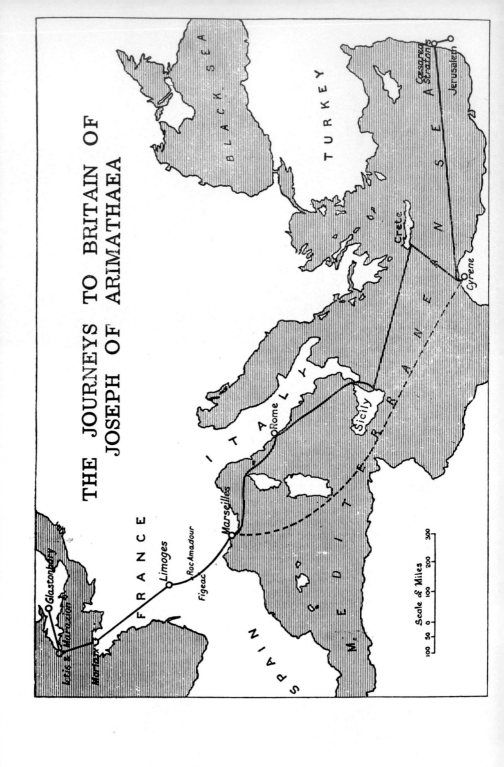

THE JOURNEYS TO BRITAIN OF JOSEPH OF ARIMATHAEA

Scale of Miles
100 50 0   100   200   300

the saying which He spake unto them. And He went down with them, and came to Nazareth, and was subject unto them: but His mother kept all these sayings in her heart. And Jesus increased in wisdom and stature, and in favour with God and man ".[2]

So there we have *the only record of Jesus' childhood.* The Bible tells us nothing more about the next eighteen years of Jesus' life until He was " about thirty years of age ",[3] and then, " Jesus also being baptized, and praying, the heaven was opened, and the Holy Ghost descended in a bodily shape like a dove upon Him, and a voice came from heaven, which said, Thou art My beloved Son; in Thee I am well pleased ".[4] At this moment in His life, Jesus being baptised, potentially laid down His life, the sacrifice being sealed with His actual death and resurrection three-and-a-half years later.

Then following His baptism, " Jesus being full of the Holy Ghost returned from Jordan, and was led by the Spirit into the wilderness, being forty days tempted of the devil ".[5] " And Jesus returned in the power of the Spirit into Galilee: and there went out a fame of Him through all the region round about. And He taught in their synagogues, being glorified of all ".[6]

Notice, while we do know that Jesus spent His early years in Nazareth, there is nothing told us of His early youth or manhood. However, certain Scriptures imply the possibility that Jesus had been away from Nazareth for some considerable time. For instance, the passage just quoted continues, " And He came to Nazareth, where He had been *brought up :* and, as His custom was, He went into the synagogue on the Sabbath day, and stood up for to read . . . and the eyes of all them that were in the synagogue were fastened on Him. And He began to say unto them, This day is this scripture fulfilled in your ears. And all bare Him witness, and wondered at the gracious words which proceeded out of His mouth. And they said, *Is not this Joseph's son? ".[7]

Two things strike us here. The Bible says, " He came to Nazareth where he had been *brought up".* The very usage of this expression implies that whilst Jesus' early life had been spent in Nazareth, *He had not continued to live there.* His more recent days had been spent elsewhere. This impression is strengthened by the fact that His hearers ask the question, " Is not this Joseph's son? ", almost as though they were *in doubt as to His identity.*

We also read that they asked, " Is not this the carpenter, the son of Mary, the brother of James, and Joses, and of Juda, and Simon? and are not His sisters here with us? ",[8] and elsewhere, " Is not this the carpenter's Son? is not His mother called Mary?

and His brethren, James, and Joses, and Simon, and Judas? And His sisters, are they not all with us?"[9] Was Jesus such a stranger to them that the people could refer to Him not by name but only by His relationship to the other members of His family?

Now notice another passage of Scripture. "And when they were come to Capernaum, they that received tribute money came to Peter, and said, Doth not your Master pay tribute? He saith, Yes. And when he was come into the house, Jesus prevented him, saying, What thinkest thou, Simon? of whom do the kings of the earth take custom or tribute? of their own children, or of strangers? Peter saith unto Him, Of strangers. Jesus saith unto him, Then are the children free. Notwithstanding, lest we should offend them, go thou to the sea, and cast an hook, and take up the fish that first cometh up; and when thou hast opened his mouth, thou shalt find a piece of money: that take, and give unto them for Me and thee ".[10]

Now we know that Jesus spent much of His time ministering in Capernaum. In fact, by comparing the account of the healing of the man sick of the palsy as recorded[11] by Matthew with that given[12] by Mark, we find that Capernaum is described as " His own city ". Yet here was an enquiry being made about Jesus' liability to the *strangers' tax*, the Greek *didrachma*, which was levied on FOREIGN visitors to Capernaum, notably traders and merchantmen who conducted their business there. Evidently there was some question in the minds of the authorities as to Jesus' liability to tax *on the grounds of His having been away.*

Jesus then enquired of Peter who were normally expected to pay custom or tribute, to which Peter replied, strangers (i.e. foreigners, the Greek word *allotrios*). Jesus said, " Then are the children free [exempt, Greek *eleutheros*] ". Then, so as not to give offence, Jesus sent Peter to catch a fish, the first one he would bring up having a coin in its mouth. This coin was the Greek *stater*, worth *twice as much* as the didrachma, sufficient to pay the tax for two people.

Of course, it may be objected that the tax in question was the Temple tax. However, unless the authorities were uncertain as to Jesus' nationality which they surely were not, there could have been no doubt that Jesus WAS liable to pay the Temple tax. Moreover, the Temple tax would have been paid with a *Jewish shekel* whereas it was a Greek coin which Jesus provided. Whichever way one looks at this incident, there is more than a suggestion that Jesus had been absent from Palestine for some considerable time.

Jesus said, " I must be about My Father's business ".[13] Now link this with His statement to the Syrophenician woman, " I am not sent but unto the lost sheep of the house of Israel ".[14] As will by now have become clear to the reader, the lost tribes of the house of Israel were already by this time becoming settled in the British Isles: some had been there for a thousand years. Is it unreasonable to believe that, should there have been an opportunity to do so, Jesus would have desired to visit the land which one day would be responsible more than any other for the proclamation of the gospel around the world?

And Jesus might easily have had that opportunity. We have already shown in Chapter Two the probable relationship of Jesus to Joseph of Arimathæa. We believe that Joseph was Jesus' great uncle. There can be little doubt whatever that Joseph was familiar with Britain and visited these Islands, and Jesus might so easily have accompanied him. This is exactly the tradition related by Baring-Gould in his *Book of Cornwall* :

" Another Cornish story is to the effect that Joseph of Arimathæa came in a boat to Cornwall and brought the child Jesus with him, and the latter taught him how to extract the tin and purge it of its wolfram. When the tin is flashed then the tinner shouts ' Joseph was in the tin trade ' " (*Page 57*).

There is also the tradition in Somerset that Joseph and Jesus " came in a ship of Tarshish to the Summerland and sojourned in a place called Paradise ". Certainly one finds the name Paradise around Burnham-on-Sea and especially around Glastonbury, and one has only to think of the proliferation of names in Somerset and Cornwall such as *Christ*on, Mara*zion*, *Jesus* Well, Port *Isaac* and *Jacobs*town to realise that the traditions may have some foundation in fact. Although we have not so far attempted to discover the derivation of these place names, cumulatively they do appear to be significant.

Then on the top of the Mendip Hills, right in the centre of the ancient lead and copper mining industry, is the little hamlet of Priddy, where people were wont to say, " *As sure as our Lord was at Priddy* ". What a very strange saying this is if, in fact, Jesus was never there. Priddy is a delightful spot—see the colour photograph facing page 85. Whenever he is in the district, the writer always makes a point of visiting the place. He drives up the long steep hill from Draycott on the Cheddar-Wells road until at the top a glorious view is spread out before one. In these quiet hills, it is not difficult to imagine Jesus being here and striding along the same pathways across the hills which must have been in use for thousands of years.

And then at the foot of the Mendips is the little village oi Pilton. It is from Pilton that the lead and copper ore which was mined in the hills used to be taken down the River Brue to Burn-ham-on-Sea. Here too a tradition has remained of Jesus having been here, and in the local Parish Church is a beautifully em-broidered flag showing Joseph of Arimathæa and Jesus arriving in a little boat.

But most of the traditions seem to be connected with Glastonbury. Certainly Glastonbury's early history suggests that the sanctity with which the place was held was due to more than Joseph's having settled there. From the earliest times two strange names have been used to describe Glastonbury, *Secretum Domini* or 'Secret of the Lord', and *Domus Dei* meaning 'Home of God', and these have been ascribed to the belief that Jesus Him-self once lived here and that in this place He constructed the building which became His home.

We have seen these traditions variously ascribed to the invention of a school mistress a century ago, or to the invention of 12th century monks seeking to enhance the reputation of their Abbey. Yet those who seek to ridicule the traditions have no alternative explanation to offer as to how and where Jesus' missing years were spent, nor can they account for the prevalence of the legend in places considerably removed from monastic influence. Nor should we arbitrarily dismiss the documentary evidence which seems to substantiate the claims that Jesus came to Britain.

For instance, the noted historian William of Malmesbury (1080-1143) quotes a letter said to have been written by Augustine to Pope Gregory, *Epistolae ad Gregorium Papam*, in which he refers to the Wattle Church at Glastonbury as having been " constructed by no human art, but by the hands of Christ Himself."

" In the western confines of Britain there is a certain royal island of large extent, surrounded by water, abounding in all the beauties of nature and necessaries of life. In it the first neophytes of the catholic law, God beforehand acquainting them, found *a Church constructed by no human art, but by the Hands of Christ Himself*, for the salvation of His people. The Almighty has made it manifest by many miracles and mysterious visitations that He continues to watch over it as sacred to Himself, and to Mary, the Mother of God ".

We may, of course, attribute the suggestion that the Lord Jesus Himself constructed the Wattle Church to wishful thinking or wilful exaggeration, but the fact remains that the Wattle Church DID exist—of this there can be no doubt—and it WAS regarded with great veneration for centuries before its final destruction in 1184.

Whatever the truth of the matter, it will be profitable for us to learn how the people of Somerset were living in Jesus' day, for nothing can be farther from the truth than that the British at this time were a race of painted savages. We now have a very accurate picture of what life must have been like in those days because in the vicinity of Glastonbury, actually at Godney and Meare, lake villages have been discovered in a perfect state of preservation.

A mass of dome-shaped hillocks, indicates the position where the dwellings stood. There were about 89 at Godney and 120 at Meare. The foundation had been laid with timber, mostly alder and oak, brushwood had been laid on top, and clay had been applied in layers for the flooring. The walls were of wattle and daub, six-foot high and vertical, and the roofs consisted of reeds and rushes, the whole edifice being supported by a central pole around which was a hearth. The wattle when uncovered was as good as new.

These villages were being lived in at the time of Christ and their discovery gives us an accurate picture of what life must have been like. The people evidently tilled the land, grew cereals and bred domestic animals, and farmed on higher ground. They were skilled weavers and potters, and worked in iron, bronze, tin and lead, and also wood. Tools and implements of bone, antler and wood have been found, also beads of glass and amber, bronze brooches, bracelets and rings, delicate fibulae (exactly like our safety-pins), and a beautiful bowl.

These, then, would have been the people amongst whom Jesus may have lived although none would have known His identity until later years. Here He may very well have spent the years of preparation for a ministry that has changed the world. But of one thing we may be certain: Jesus would not have performed miracles in Britain, for it was not until His baptism by John and His receiving the power of the Holy Spirit that He commenced His public ministry.

The Bible speaks of " all that Jesus BEGAN both to do and teach ".[15] It tells us, concerning His changing the water into wine, " This BEGINNING of miracles did Jesus in Cana of Galilee, and manifested forth His glory ".[16] There are numerous apocryphal New Testament books in existence which relate childhood miracles which Jesus is supposed to have performed, but these are clearly spurious as will be immediately obvious by their weird and unspiritual nature, for instance the infant Jesus allegedly bringing clay animals and birds to life.[17]

The tradition that Jesus came to Britain may very well be true. The absence of much written confirmation is only what might be expected in the circumstances. Jesus' hidden years were undoubtedly years of preparation. They would have been spent in relative obscurity. He would not have engaged in public ministry. There would have been nothing spectacular about Jesus to have drawn attention to Him. Only in later years, after the Crucifixion and Resurrection and Ascension, and the coming of Joseph of Arimathǽa to preach in this land, would people have learned who Jesus really was.

Whether Jesus came and lived in Britain is immaterial. What really matters is that Christ lives today in the hearts of His people. Whether Jesus did once walk upon the Mendip hills we do not know. What is really important is that He has promised, " I will dwell in them, and walk in them; and I will be their God, and they shall be My people ".[18] This, we suggest, is the greatest privilege on earth.

[1] Deuteronomy 12: 11
[2] Luke 2: 41-52
[3] Luke 3: 23
[4] Luke 3: 21-22
[5] Luke 4: 1-2
[6] Luke 4: 14-15
[7] Luke 4: 16-22
[8] Mark 6: 3
[9] Matthew 13: 55-56
[10] Matthew 17: 24-27
[11] Matthew 9: 1
[12] Mark 2: 1
[13] Luke 2: 49
[14] Matthew 15: 24
[15] Acts 1: 1
[16] John 2: 11
[17] 1 Infancy 15: 1-6
      (Apoc. N.T.)
[18] 2 Corinthians 6: 16

CHAPTER NINE

GOD'S CHOSEN PEOPLE

WE have seen that the gospel came to Britain in the very earliest days and quite possibly the Lord Jesus Christ Himself visited this land. We have shown that the first people in the world *nationally* to become Christian were the British, and we have spoken of the part played by the Church in the development of the British character with its ideals of duty, freedom and service. The question we have to ask is, Why has this been so? If, as the Bible says, "the Most High ruleth in the kingdom of men",[1] then, surely, in our nation's history we should see the outworking of divine providence.

This brings us to consider the whole plan of God as revealed to us in the Holy Bible. Briefly stated, that plan may be said to be the calling out, training and preparation of a special people as the instrument in God's hand of blessing the whole world.

God has a plan for this world. That plan embraces every human being who has ever lived. Its comprehensive purpose may be discerned from many passages of Scripture:

" [God] will have ALL MEN to be saved, and to come unto the knowledge of the truth ".[2]

" God . . . is the Saviour of ALL MEN, specially of those that believe ".[3]

" For the grace of God hath appeared bringing salvation to ALL MEN ".[4]

" And I, if I be lifted up from the earth, will draw ALL MEN unto Me ".[5]

We might quote dozens of other scriptures which establish this glorious truth. Suffice it to say that God has promised to bless ALL families,[6] ALL people,[7] ALL nations,[8] ALL the world,[9]

67

ALL creation[10] and ALL things.[11] This will come about through the return of the Lord Jesus Christ to set up His Kingdom upon the earth and to rule the world.

This good news is what we call the *gospel*. In order that men might believe the good news, Jesus said that " this gospel of the kingdom shall be preached in all the world for a witness unto all nations; and then shall the end [of the age] come ".[12] Therefore a people had to be brought into existence which would not only preach but *demonstrate* the message of the Kingdom. There had to be a nation which would live by the faith of Christ, keeping His laws and teaching the rest of mankind the way to true peace, happiness and prosperity, a nation which would give Christian civilisation to the world.

That nation was Israel. But before the nation could come into existence God first of all chose a man. His name was Abraham. The Bible tells us, " Now the LORD had said unto Abram, Get thee out of thy country, and from thy kindred, and from thy father's house, unto a land that I will shew thee: and I will make of thee a GREAT NATION, and I will bless thee, and make thy name great; and thou shalt be a blessing: and I will bless them that bless thee, and curse him that curseth thee: *and in thee shall all families of the earth be blessed* ".[13]

This promise now became unconditional, " By Myself have I sworn, saith the LORD, for because thou hast done this thing, and hast not withheld thy son, thine only son: that in blessing I will bless thee, and in multiplying I will multiply thy seed as the stars of the heaven, and as the sand which is upon the sea shore; and thy seed shall possess the gate of his enemies; *and in thy seed shall all the nations of the earth be blessed;* because thou hast obeyed My voice ".[14]

The promise was repeated to Isaac and Jacob. It was reiterated and enlarged upon, the chosen people revealed as " spread[ing] abroad to the west, and to the east, and to the north, and to the south ",[15] to become, " in the last days ",[16] " A NATION and a COMPANY [COMMONWEALTH] OF NATIONS ".[17]

The covenant was confirmed to Jacob in 1883 B.C. Four hundred and thirty years later the Lord brought Israel out of bondage in Egypt and gave them His law. He told them through Moses, " Ye have seen what I did unto the Egyptians, and how I bare you on eagles' wings, and brought you unto Myself. Now therefore, if ye will obey My voice indeed, and keep My covenant, then ye shall be a PECULIAR TREASURE unto Me above all people: for all the earth is Mine: and ye shall be unto Me a KINGDOM OF PRIESTS, and an HOLY NATION ".[18]

GLASTONBURY ABBEY

The photograph shows all that remains of the nave and choir of the Great Church; St. Joseph's Chapel is not shown. The lower picture shows how the Abbey would have appeared before its destruction in 1539.

THE GARDEN OF CHALICE WELL

From the Well the water is piped down the terraced garden, gushing forth from a low wall where all may drink. The garden is alive with the sound and sparkle of moving water.

Over and over again Israel was reminded that they were GOD'S CHOSEN PEOPLE. " For thou art an holy people unto the LORD thy God, and the LORD hath chosen thee to be a PECULIAR PEOPLE unto Himself, above all the nations that are upon the earth ".[19] Moses reminded the people, " For what nation is there so great, who hath God so nigh unto them, as the LORD our God is in all things that we call upon Him for? And what nation is there so great, that hath statutes and judgments so righteous as all this law, which I set before you this day? "[20]

So the Lord made a covenant with Israel whereby they became His people. But this covenant, the Mosaic (because it was given through Moses), was conditional upon Israel's obedience. Notice the condition, " If ye will . . . keep My covenant, then ye shall be [MY] PEOPLE ". The Mosaic covenant with Israel was made conditional upon their keeping the Law. When Israel broke the Law they forfeited the right to call themselves God's people. *But that could not nullify the covenant which God made with Abraham, Isaac and Jacob* because this was UNCONDITIONAL. " And this I say, that the covenant [made with Abraham, Isaac and Jacob] that was confirmed before of God in Christ, *the law, which was four hundred and thirty years after, cannot disannul, that it should make the promise of none effect* ".[21]

So God must find a way whereby He may fulfil His promises to Abraham and so bless all families and all nations of the world, but at the same time do so through a people, Israel, who have forfeited all right to be known as His people![22]

God cannot change His plan. He cannot give up Israel. He cannot (despite what some theologians would say) start a Church to perform the task which Israel was given to do. He cannot do any of these things because He has sworn by Himself.[23] Moreover, He has promised that Israel shall be a people unto Him FOR EVER.

Notice David's prayer, " And what one nation in the earth is like THY PEOPLE, even like ISRAEL, whom God went to redeem for a people to Himself, and to make Him a name, and to do for you great things and terrible, for Thy land, before THY PEOPLE, which Thou redeemedst to Thee from Egypt, from the nations and their gods? For Thou hast confirmed to Thyself THY PEOPLE ISRAEL to be *a people unto Thee for ever :* and Thou, LORD, art become their God ".[24]

Again the Bible tells us, " Thus saith the LORD, which giveth the sun for a light by day, and the ordinances of the moon and of the stars for a light by night, which divideth the sea when the waves thereof roar; The LORD of hosts is His name: If those ordinances depart from before Me, saith the LORD, then the seed of Israel also shall cease from being a nation before Me for ever. Thus saith the LORD; If heaven above can be measured, and the foundations of the earth searched out beneath, I will also cast off all the seed of Israel for all that they have done, saith the LORD ".[25] Israel was to be a NATION as long as the sun, moon and stars should last. God would always have a CHOSEN PEOPLE.

Clearly, the old (Mosaic) covenant was abrogated and a new covenant required. But this new covenant would have to be a covenant in which God would take the initiative and which Israel could keep, and for that to be possible Israel would need to receive divine help—they would need the power of the Holy Spirit to enable them to keep God's laws and to become once again a people demonstrating the divine purposes.

So the Lord announced through Jeremiah, " Behold, the days come, saith the LORD, that I will make a *new covenant* with the house of Israel, and with the house of Judah: not according to the covenant that I made with their fathers in the day that I took them by the hand to bring them out of the land of Egypt; which My covenant they brake, although I was an husband unto them, saith the LORD: but this shall be the covenant that I will make with the house of Israel; After those days, saith the LORD, I will *put My law in their inward parts*, and *write it in their hearts;* and will be their God, and they shall be MY PEOPLE. And they shall teach no more every man his neighbour, and every man his brother, saying, Know the LORD: for they shall all know Me, from the least of them unto the greatest of them, saith the LORD; for I will forgive their iniquity, and I will remember their sin no more ".[26]

So the Lord promised that a new covenant would be made with the house of Israel whereby they would once again become His people and He would be their God. In the meantime, however, until that time should come, the house of Israel was taken captive into Assyria,[27] 735-670 B.C., never returning to the land of Palestine,[28] and ultimately becoming known as " the lost sheep of the house of Israel ".[29] Israel had forfeited the right to be known as God's people. Now they would be NOT-MY-PEOPLE. Even so, there was a promise of restoration to become once again MY PEOPLE.

Notice, " Then said God, Call his name Lo-ammi: for ye are NOT MY PEOPLE, and I will not be your God. Yet the number of the children of Israel shall be as the sand of the sea, which cannot be measured nor numbered; and it shall come to pass, that in the place where it was said unto them, Ye are not My people, there it shall be said unto them, Ye are the SONS OF THE LIVING GOD ".[30] It is Christians who are known as " the sons of God ",[31] so Israel was to become CHRISTIAN!

The house of Judah was also taken captive into Babylon, 604-595 B.C., a tiny portion of these Judah people returning to their homeland 70 years later to become known as the Jews.

To this Jewish people came the Lord Jesus Christ as their promised Messiah, the One who by His atoning death and resurrection would institute the new covenant. At the Last Supper, on the evening before His crucifixion, " as they were eating, Jesus took bread, and blessed it, and brake it, and gave it to the disciples, and said, Take, eat; this is My body. And He took the cup, and gave thanks, and gave it to them, saying, Drink ye all of it; for this is My blood of the new testament, which is shed for many for the remission of sins ".[32]

The only way whereby Israel could enter this new covenant relationship was by having their sins forgiven, for " without shedding of blood there is no remission ".[33] But the only sufficient sacrifice was the sinless, spotless Son of God Himself, because if a sinner had died he would have paid the just penalty of the Law but could never have atoned for his own or another's sins.

So the Lord Jesus Christ died as a sacrifice for sin so that Israel might be redeemed—brought back into covenant relationship with Himself. But the Jews refused to accept the person and mission of the Lord Jesus Christ. It was, ironically, they who put Him to death.

Now we see that Jesus' death was the means whereby the new testament could be brought into effect. " For where a testament is, there must also of necessity be the death of the testator. For a testament is of force after men are dead: otherwise it is of no strength at all while the testator liveth ".[34] Obviously, a person's last will and testament cannot come into force until that person is dead. Jesus died, and so the new testament could come into effect. Moreover, since Jesus rose from the dead, those who were to come under this new covenant could receive the Holy Spirit, thus enabling them to live by God's law which had been the condition of the old covenant!

Now Jesus knew that the Jews would reject Him: it was part of the " determinate counsel and foreknowledge of God ".[35] And before His death He told the Jews, " Therefore say I unto you, The kingdom of God shall be taken from you, and given to a NATION bringing forth the fruits thereof ".[36] The Lord had promised unconditionally to bless the world through the descendants of Abraham, Isaac and Jacob, through ISRAEL. That promise could now begin to be fulfilled through that other part of God's chosen people, the ten-tribed house of Israel who had long ago gone into captivity, but were now to be reformed as a CHRISTIAN NATION. Through the ministry of the Apostles, the dispersed tribes of Israel would begin to accept the Lord Jesus Christ as their Redeemer, and would become a CHRISTIAN people.

Now they would once again become GOD'S CHOSEN PEOPLE. Notice that Peter, writing to " the strangers [God's Israel people in dispersion] scattered throughout Pontus, Galatia, Cappadocia, Asia, and Bithynia "[37] says, " But ye are a CHOSEN GENERATION, a ROYAL PRIESTHOOD, an HOLY NATION, a PECULIAR PEOPLE; that ye should shew forth the praises [margin, *virtues*] of Him who hath called you out of darkness into His marvellous light: which in time past were NOT A PEOPLE, but are now the PEOPLE OF GOD: which had not obtained mercy, but now have obtained mercy ".[38]

God still has a chosen people. That chosen people is ISRAEL. The chosen people could only be used of God through its *national* acceptance of the Lord Jesus Christ. Therefore Israel had to become a CHRISTIAN NATION. Israel today is a Christian nation, and *that nation is Britain and all its kindred peoples.*

Now we are in a position to see what lies behind the marvellous story we have to tell. God has a plan to bless the world. He has planned to bless the world through Christ. A nation must be formed to give Christ to the world and that nation is Israel. Britain *is* Israel, therefore it must become a Christian nation giving Christian civilisation to the world. No wonder then that the Apostles should come to Britain. No wonder that the gospel should from the very first receive Royal patronage. No wonder that the Church in these islands should be the oldest in the world. No wonder that Britain should have become the greatest nation on the face of the earth, with an Empire upon which the sun never set.

We repeat, *God still has a chosen people.* That people has been chosen for service. That does not mean to say that God is not interested in any other people, but rather the very opposite. He has chosen one nation, Israel, so that *through Israel's God—* THE LORD JESUS CHRIST HIMSELF—*all nations might be blessed.* The one nation which has given Jesus Christ to the world is Britain, and, of course, America which was peopled from British stock.

Israel today is a Christian nation. That is not to say that all of its people are soundly converted, God-saved, Spirit-begotten children of God. In Bible days Israel was very far from being a godly nation. We have only to remember Israel's idolatry—the pagan sun-worship of which we spoke in Chapter Three—to realise this. Today as a nation we are sadly fallen from grace, but we are still GOD'S CHOSEN PEOPLE with a task to fulfil.

But, of course, God's offer of salvation is for ALL MEN[39] irrespective of nationality, colour or class. The moment a person receives the Lord Jesus Christ as his very own Saviour that person becomes an Israelite! " And if ye be Christ's, then are ye Abraham's seed, and heirs according to the promise ".[40]

Thus it has fallen to the British and American people to give Christianity to the world. Britain, the Commonwealth and the United States of America, are the world's centre and nucleus of Christianity, the custodians of the Word of God, and the propagators of the gospel to the nations of the world. It is we who have translated the Bible into almost a thousand tongues. It is we who have been responsible for more than 90 per cent. of all missionary activity.

The only reason why the world and even Britain herself does not know that she is Israel is that God planned it that way. Despite the fact that the British people worship in their National Church as though they were Israel (see Chapter Eleven), and despite the fact that our people have fulfilled exactly what was promised through Israel, the nation is still blind to its identity and shall be until that day when God takes the blindness away.

[1] Daniel 4: 25
[2] 1 Timothy 2: 4
[3] 1 Timothy 4: 10
[4] Titus 2: 11 (R.V.)
[5] John 12: 32
[6] Genesis 28: 14
[7] Luke 2: 10
[8] Psalm 72: 17
[9] John 12: 47
[10] Revelation 5: 13
[11] Colossians 1: 20
[12] Matthew 24: 14
[13] Genesis 12: 1-3
[14] Genesis 22: 16-18
[15] Genesis 28: 14
[16] Genesis 49: 1
[17] Genesis 35: 11
[18] Exodus 19: 4-6
[19] Deuteronomy 14: 2
[20] Deuteronomy 4: 7-8
[21] Galatians 3: 17
[22] Hosea 1: 9
[23] Hebrews 6: 13
[24] 2 Samuel 7: 23-24
[25] Jeremiah 31: 35-37
[26] Jeremiah 31: 31-34
[27] 2 Kings 17: 6
[28] 2 Kings 17: 23
[29] Matthew 10: 6
[30] Hosea 1: 9-10
[31] John 1: 12
[32] Matthew 26: 26-28
[33] Hebrews 9: 22
[34] Hebrews 9: 16-17
[35] Acts 2: 23
[36] Matthew 21: 43
[37] 1 Peter 1: 1
[38] 1 Peter 2: 9-10
[39] Acts 2: 21
[40] Galatians 3: 29

CHAPTER TEN

THE MIRACLE OF THE HOLY THORN

I AM writing this on Glastonbury's Wearyall Hill on a sunny afternoon in May. Down below me the main road runs to Street and Taunton, while away to my right is the mass of red roofs which is Glastonbury. I can clearly see the ruins of the Abbey about half-a-mile away.

A few yards further down the hill is the Holy Thorn tree, said to mark the exact spot where Joseph of Arimathæa planted his staff all those years ago, while beyond that Hill Head curves away into the distance with the little cottage where we are staying just out of sight.

When I climbed the hill this morning in the first light of day, the whole area was swathed in mist and the road below was lost to view. I wondered if perhaps it had been the same when Joseph and his little party arrived here so many years ago. They journeyed here by boat and then would have climbed the hill, and " weary all " with their journey would have sat down to rest. Of course, the name ' Wearyall ' has nothing to do with the fatigue of Joseph and his companions. It is simply a form of the Celtic word, *Wirral*, meaning a peninsula or promontory. It is easy to see that centuries ago until the water receded, Wearyall or Wirral Hill would have been a tongue of land protruding into the sea.

According to the legend, the staff which Joseph planted in the ground took root and sprang up overnight. Whether there is any truth in this we cannot say. It is certainly not unknown for a staff cut from a tree to take root, and the Bible tells of Aaron's rod which budded. " And Moses spake unto the children of Israel, and every one of their princes gave him a rod apiece, for each prince one, according to their fathers' houses, even twelve

74

rods: and the rod of Aaron was among their rods. And Moses laid up the rods before the LORD in the tabernacle of witness. And it came to pass, that on the morrow Moses went into the tabernacle of witness; and, behold, the rod of Aaron for the house of Levi was budded, and brought forth buds, and bloomed blossoms, and yielded almonds ".[1]

Set in the ground beside the thorn tree is a stone slab with the inscription " J.A. Anno D. XXXI " which was placed there by one John Clark. The J.A. refers, obviously, to Joseph of Arimathæa, but the date given, A.D. 31, is incorrect as the Crucifixion did not take place until A.D. 33. The mistake seems to have come about by a misreading of a bronze tablet which was formerly placed in the Abbey church. This read, " In the year XXXI after the Lord's passion, twelve holy men, of whom Joseph of Arimathæa was the chief, came hither and built the first church of this kingdom, in this place which Christ at this time dedicated to the honour of His Mother and as a place for their burial." Thirty-one years after the Lord's passion would be A.D. 64 which has been suggested as an alternative date for Joseph's coming.

This thorn has engaged the attention of botanists for the past four centuries. It is a species *Crataegus monogyna praecox* which was common in Palestine but is unique in that it flowers twice a year, in May—this one has a few blooms now—and again at Christmas, supposedly in honour of Christ's birthday. For many centuries the blooming of the thorn at Christmas was regarded as a miracle, and the tree was studied very closely in 1752 when Christmas Day was changed.

What had happened was this. In 1582 Pope Gregory XIII introduced a new calendar. The Julian calendar (named after Julius Caesar) which had been in use until that time was found to be several days out, so ten days were omitted from the calendar that year, and the day following October 4th was called October 15th. (The day of the week, incidentally, did NOT change.) October 4th was a Thursday but the following day, now called October 15th, was still a Friday.) However, so great was the theological bitterness of the day that protestant countries refused to accept the Pope's ruling, and England retained the old calendar.

A further 170 years passed. By now the discrepancy between the sun and the Julian calendar still in use in England had increased to 11 days and in 1752 the new Gregorian calendar had to be accepted. September 2nd was followed by September 14th. (Again, there was no alteration in the *order* of the days of the week: September 2nd was a Wednesday and the next day, September 14th, was a Thursday.) Great was the interest to see whether the holy thorn would sanction the change in the calendar. Not very surprisingly the thorn did not burst into flower until the following 6th January!

The thorn still flowers during the Christmas season. But one thing is certain. December 25th was not the birthday of Jesus and certainly would not have been celebrated by Joseph of Arimathæa. It was never observed by the early Church but had its origin in paganism. For long centuries before the Christian era, December 25th was celebrated in honour of Nimrod or the devil.

Nimrod was the son of Cush,² who was the son of Ham,³ who was cursed by his father Noah.⁴ It was Nimrod who built Babel or Babylon, "And the beginning of his kingdom was Babel ".⁵ All through the Bible this Babylon is the counterfeit of the Kingdom of God, the personification of everything that is corrupt and evil and contrary to God.

Nimrod was so evil that he married his own mother whose name was Semiramis. After his untimely death, Semiramis made believe that her son had been miraculously raised from the dead, a counterfeit of the Resurrection of Christ. She claimed that a dead tree stump had miraculously sprung to life as a full-grown evergreen, and that to prove that Nimrod was alive again, every year on the anniversary of his birth, her son would leave gifts on the fir tree. *Nimrod's birthday was 25th December!*

So the Christmas tree has its origin in paganism, but that is not all. Semiramis claimed that Nimrod her son had been virgin-born and that Baal the sun-god was his father. So it was not long before Semiramis was worshipped as the "Queen of Heaven "⁶ with Nimrod a false messiah. This was how the cult of mother and child originated, the "Madonna and Child" of Roman Catholicism. Moreover, Nimrod's birthday, December 25th, continued to be observed all down the centuries in honour of the sun-god. It was a night of revelry and drunken debauchery, and when Simon Magus established a counterfeit church at Rome (see page 12) and the Babylonian Mystery Religion was dressed up as 'Christianity', Christmas was incorporated into the Christian calendar.

But sun worship was no new thing even for God's Israel people. As we showed in Chapter Three, Israel had turned to idolatry and sun worship long before the Assyrian captivity (735-670 B.C.) And when they migrated to Britain as Celts with the Druidic religion, they celebrated the death of the old sun and the birth of the new sun at the winter solstice, the shortest day

BRITISH STONE CIRCLES

Stonehenge, Wiltshire, Europe's finest Bronze Age monument, dating from 1800 B.C., and, below, the Rollright Stones in Oxfordshire.

THE HOLY THORN ON WEARYALL

Here Joseph of Arimathæa is said to have planted his staff which took root and grew into a tree. The thorn blossoms twice a year, at Christmas and again in May.

of the year. The mistletoe was considered sacred to the sun, and so became identified with the festivities of Christmas.

But the true Church of God in Bible days never observed Christmas. It became universally observed only when ' Christianity' became the state religion of the Roman Empire under Constantine in the year 312. Now see what God says about decorating the Christmas tree. " Hear ye the word which the LORD speaketh unto you, O house of Israel: Thus saith the LORD, Learn not the way of the heathen, and be not dismayed at the signs of heaven; for the heathen are dismayed at them. For the customs of the people are vain: for one cutteth a tree out of the forest, the work of the hands of the workman, with the axe. They deck it with silver and with gold; they fasten it with nails and with hammers, that it move not. They are upright as the palm tree, but speak not: they must needs be borne, because they cannot go. Be not afraid of them; for they cannot do evil, neither also is it in them to do good ".[7]

So the thorn tree on Wearyall flowered at Christmas and still does so today, but not in honour of Christ's birthday, and the Bible tells us " Neither give heed to fables ".[8] We do not even know exactly when Christ was born, but evidently it could not have been in December for the Bible says that when Mary " brought forth her firstborn son, and wrapped Him in swaddling clothes, and laid Him in a manger; because there was no room for them in the inn . . . there were in the same country shepherds abiding in the field, keeping watch over their flock by night ".[9] The flocks would not have been out in the fields by night during the cold rainy winter; they were taken indoors probably not later than October.

But perhaps it is a miracle that the thorn tree should have survived at all. It has stood for many centuries on Wearyall, and is mentioned in a book on Joseph of Arimathæa written by Richard Pynson, a pupil of William Caxton, in 1520. In the time of Queen Elizabeth I (1558-1603) it was a sturdy tree with a twin trunk and strong branches. Then during the days of the Commonwealth (1649-1660) when Charles I was deposed and Oliver Cromwell ruled England, a fanatical puritan attempted to destroy it with a hatchet. He had successfully cut down one of its two trunks and was attacking the other one when a splinter flew into his eye, causing him to leave off. The tree ultimately died although a stump remained even in 1740, but cuttings made from the original tree still flourished, and today the thorn on Wearyall Hill is one sprung from the original and grows on the same spot. There is another thorn tree in the grounds of the Abbey, and a fine specimen in the church of St. John's in Glastonbury High Street.

The thorn still flowers during the Christmas season, and in 1929 the custom was revived of sending a sprig of flowers to the Sovereign, with greetings from the Mayor and Vicar. Her Majesty the Queen receives a sprig from the tree every year.

In a curious way then, this thorn tree is symbolic of the continuing faith of Christ in Britain and its patronage by the Royal House (see page 51) all down the centuries. And the story of the Church in Glastonbury is the story of the faith in England. What an amazing story that has been.

Arviragus gave Joseph and his companions twelve hides of land and they built the Wattle Church. They built for themselves wattle huts around the stream which is now known as Chalice Well. There they lived and ministered and died, their places being taken by other anchorites as time passed.

In the year A.D. 166, Eleutherius, at the request of King Lucius, sent two missionaries Fagan and Dyfan to Britain, who are said to have rebuilt the Wattle Church. It became the repository of many saints.

In the fifth century St. Patrick visited Glastonbury and is said to have become its first Abbot c. 450. He died in 461.

King Arthur was buried at Glastonbury in 540; the remains of his shrine were discovered as recently as 1934.

In 633 Paulinus the companion of Augustine covered the Wattle Church with wood and encased it in lead. In 688 King Ina of Wessex built and endowed a monastery. The text of the Abbey's charter, about 704, still exists, confirming to the church certain rites and possessions which it previously held. It was King Ina who built the greater church in honour of Peter and Paul, and Ina who handed Glastonbury to Rome in 725.

Dunstan, who was born at nearby Baltonsborough and educated at the monastery, was made Abbot of Glastonbury by King Eadmund in 943. It has been spoken of as a turning point in the history of religion in England. He introduced the Benedictine rule into the monastic house, and Glastonbury entered upon a golden era of political and literary activity; its school was the most famous in England. Dunstan became Archbishop of Canterbury.

The first Norman Abbot began to build a new and finer church; the second pulled it down and built another which was the finest in England, 1101-1120. It housed a library which must have been one of the most valuable in the world. William of Malmesbury came to Glastonbury in 1125 to write its history, a work which survives today only in a later and much interpolated edition.

And then came the great fire of 25th May, 1184, and the Wattle Church was destroyed. Henry II began rebuilding. The Norman Chapel of St. Mary was built on the same site and completed by 11th June, 1186. Then work commenced on the church of St. Peter and St. Paul, but as Richard I (Cœur-de-lion) was engaged in his crusades no money was available and it was a century before the work was completed. About the year 1190, the remains of King Arthur and Queen Guinevere were found. They were interred before the High Altar of the new church in 1278, and were visited by Edward I and Eleanor that year.

The history of the Abbey ended with the dissolution of the Monasteries in 1539. Commissioners were sent to the Abbey to inspect the establishment and reported well of it but an excuse was required for its suppression. The Abbot, Richard Whiting, had taken the oath of loyalty, but was arrested at his manor, taken to the Tower of London and there imprisoned. The order was given that he be returned to Glastonbury and there be tried and executed. The 80-years-old Abbot was placed on a hurdle, dragged through the town and thence to the top of Glastonbury Tor where he was hanged with two of his monks. We gloss over the horrific details; Whiting's execution has been described as " the blackest day in the Reformation ".

The Abbey was now ruthlessly pillaged and plundered and its proud walls blasted into ruin. There was a feeble though unsuccessful attempt to restore Abbey life during the brief reign of Mary (1553-1558).

John Wesley must have seen the Abbey ruins when he visited Glastonbury on 23rd September, 1756.

The Abbey now passed through many hands. At one time the ruins were used as a quarry to provide road materials.

Then on June 6th, 1907, the ruins were purchased on behalf of the Church of England for the sum of £30,000. On 22nd June, 1909, the Prince of Wales (later King George V) attended a special service there. And now, as we said at the beginning of this book, an annual pilgrimage takes place here on the last Saturday in June. Meanwhile excavations still continue, and more of Glastonbury's historic past is brought to light.

And so today, having endured the weather and storms and the violence of many generations, Glastonbury Abbey still stands. And the thorn still blooms on Wearyall.

[1] Numbers 17: 6-8   [4] Genesis 9: 20-25   [7] Jeremiah 10: 1-5
[2] Genesis 10: 8   [5] Genesis 10: 10   [8] 1 Timothy 1: 4
[3] Genesis 6: 10   [6] Jeremiah 44: 17, 25 [9] Luke 2: 7-8

CHAPTER ELEVEN

OUR HERITAGE IN THE PRAYER BOOK

WE have already spoken of the great part played by the Church in the building of the nation and the development of the national character (see page 58), and we have shown something of the continuity of the faith in these islands. This brings us to consider the liturgy of the Church and especially the Book of Common Prayer.

Outside the Bible there is no more inspired book than the Book of Common Prayer. It is based upon the pure Word of God and was authorised by King and Parliament as the nation's manual of worship. The Prayer Book is an affirmation of our *national* faith. It presents to us not merely a Church at prayer but a *nation*, and sets forth in clearest terms the Israel identity of our people. The purpose of the Prayer Book is to bring our people to a knowledge of their *national redemption* by Christ Jesus. Thus it constantly affirms that "We are His people ", " whom Thou hast redeemed with Thy precious blood ", and so on. But it also sets forth Jesus Christ as the *Saviour of the World*, showing that salvation is for all men, irrespective of nationality, race or colour. The very first words of the opening service in the Prayer Book read, "When the wicked man turneth away from his wickedness that he hath committed, and doeth that which is lawful and right, he shall save his soul alive ".[1]

It is often assumed that in the early days of the Church there was no set form of worship, there being only simple forms of prayer, but our Prayer Book is proof to the contrary. In 1549 Archbishop Cranmer stated before Parliament that the prayers which were then being incorporated in the Book of Common Prayer had been in use in Britain for 1,500 years. This means that the prayers must have originated when the faith was first planted here by Joseph of Arimathæa.

That set forms of prayer were in use from the earliest times is shown by the fact that Justin Martyr (died 155) speaks of ' common prayers ', Origen (185-254) of ' appointed prayers ' and Cyprian (died 257) of ' customary prayers '. There is a liturgy ascribed to James which was in use in Jerusalem in the third century, another of Mark used in the Church of Alexandria, another of Chrysostom in the Church of Constantinople, and various other liturgies belonging to churches widely separated. This suggests that they must have originated in a common source, which we reasonably presume to have been the Apostles themselves.

It seems unlikely that having founded churches far and wide the Apostles left them without any instruction as to the conduct of public worship or the administration of the Sacraments. Notice that Paul says, " I exhort therefore, that, first of all, supplications, prayers, intercessions, and giving of thanks, be made for all men; for kings, and for all that are in authority . . . ".[2] He also sets forth a threefold expression of church worship, " Be filled with the Spirit; speaking to yourselves in *psalms* and *hymns* and *spiritual songs*, singing and making melody in your heart to the Lord ".[3] " Let the word of Christ dwell in you richly in all wisdom; teaching and admonishing one another in *psalms* and *hymns* and *spiritual songs*, singing with grace in your hearts to the Lord ".[4] So today in the Prayer Book we have the *psalter, liturgical hymns* such as the Gloria in Excelsis, and metrical *songs*.

There are those who will question the spiritual value of set forms of prayer. They will quote the Scripture where Jesus said, " But when ye pray, use not vain repetitions, as the heathen do";' for they think that they shall be heard for their much speaking. Be not ye therefore like unto them: for your Father knoweth what things ye have need of, before ye ask Him ",[5] and then follow the familiar words of the Lord's Prayer. Opponents of set prayer would say that the Lord's Prayer was not meant to be repeated but intended only as a general pattern of prayer, " *After this manner* therefore pray ye: Our Father which art in heaven . . . ".[6] Yet notice Luke's account. " And it came to pass, that, as He was praying in a certain place, when He ceased, one of His disciples said unto Him, Lord, teach us to pray, *as John also taught his disciples* ". (Does this suggest that John may have given some set form of prayer to his followers?) " And He said unto them, *When ye pray*, say, Our Father which art in heaven . . . ".[7] Notice that whereas Matthew records Jesus as saying " *after this manner* . . . pray ye ", Luke says, " *when ye pray* . . . ". This suggests that the Lord's Prayer was intended for constant use. Certainly the early Church seems to have interpreted it as such. Tertullian (155-222) refers to it as "the ordinary prayer which is to be said before our other prayers, and upon which, as a foundation, our other prayers are to be built ", and tells us " the use of it was ordained by Christ ". The Lord's Prayer is mentioned also by Cyprian, Cyril, Chrysostom (347-407) and Augustine of Hippo (354-430), and many others.

The writer recognises, of course, the need and place for extempore prayer. Every Christian should be able to offer up prayer from the heart. The Bible says, " Pray without ceasing ",[8] " praying always with all prayer and supplication in the Spirit ",[9] " pray with the Spirit, and . . . pray with the understanding also ".[10] Prayer should be the natural function of every child of God. (Write for our FREE book *Healing from Christ* which deals at some length with the subject of prayer).

However, that is not to say that there is no place for the set form of prayer embodied in the Book of Common Prayer. It has a number of advantages. A condition of *common* prayer is that we know beforehand what we are praying about. There is also a great sense of the *unity* of the Church when one realises that Christians around the world, certainly in the Anglican Communion, are praying in the same words, and an awareness of the *continuity* of the Church when one knows that these words have been used by Christians in every century.

Another advantage of using a prescribed form of prayer is that the worship of the Church is not unduly affected by the minister. If praying extempore, the minister might omit something of importance or unduly repeat himself or give undue prominence to something of his special concern. The congregation, dependent upon the memory, mood and delivery of the minister, might easily be distracted. The fact that a congregation is familiar with the words to be used means that each may prepare his heart to pray and worship in the Spirit. Again we emphasise that the Book of Common Prayer is not meant to supersede spontaneous prayer on the part of the individual. It is primarily the Book of *Common* Prayer, designed for corporate use. If it be argued that set prayers are liable to mechanical repetition in which the mind is dulled, then we should point out that the Prayer Book is a marvellous blending of praise and petition in which the position of the worshipper is constantly changed by kneeling, standing and sitting.

But perhaps the greatest value of the Prayer Book is that these set prayers are thoroughly scriptural. One wonders how often this may be said of extempore prayer. The Book of Common Prayer embodies all the great Articles of our Christian faith, the teaching and practice of the Church in the age of its greatest purity and power. It is therefore a means both of teaching and also of safeguarding doctrine. And never has there been a time when it was so important for the Church to " hold fast the profession of [the] faith without wavering,"[11] and to " earnestly contend for the faith which was once delivered unto the saints ".[12] The Prayer Book is the product of the piety and spiritual devotion of men who died for the truths they stood for. How tragic therefore that clergy within the National Church have foisted upon their people a new mode of worship lacking both in grace and spirituality, with neither shape nor beauty, and so capable of any interpretation as to be bereft of any true meaning whatever. We shall have more to say about this in our closing Chapter.

The Prayer Book, then, embodies the scriptural truths as to our national identity and our place in the world. When once this great truth is understood the Book of Common Prayer becomes a never ending source of joy and wonder. Those who compiled its liturgy, and we have seen that it dates from the earliest centuries of the Christian era, clearly understood the scriptural identity of our people. In founding the British Church the Apostles prepared its services as for the worship of the Israel nation. How truly we may say then, " For the prophecy came not in old time by the will of man: but holy men of God spake as they were moved by the Holy Ghost ".[13]

Now let us look briefly at some of the features of the Prayer Book. The first service is the Order for Morning Prayer, daily throughout the year. We have already noted that the very first sentence is an injunction to the wicked man to " turn away from his wickedness that he hath committed . . . and save his soul alive ". Then in the General Confession we acknowledge, " Almighty and most merciful Father; we have erred and strayed from Thy ways like LOST SHEEP . . .". The only people which, as a nation, could justifiably refer to itself as ' lost sheep ' is Israel. Isaiah, the great prophet of Israel, says, " All we like SHEEP have gone astray; we have turned every one to his own way; and the LORD hath laid on Him the iniquity of us all ".[14] Jesus said, " I am not sent but unto the LOST SHEEP of the house of Israel ",[15] while Peter tells us, " for ye were as SHEEP going astray; but are now returned unto the Shepherd and Bishop of your souls ".[16]

Again, we confess, " we have offended against Thy holy laws " and we are reminded that " sin is the transgression of the law ",[17] and that the Law was given to Israel.[18] Then in the Absolution[19] the minister says, " God hath given power and commandment to His ministers to declare and pronounce to HIS PEOPLE, being penitent, the absolution and remission of their sins ". Notice that the minister speaks of ' Thy people ', God's people. The only *nation* which can claim to be God's people is Israel. As we showed on page 70, God said of Israel, " Call his name Lo-ammi: for ye are not My people, and I will not be your God. Yet . . . it shall come to pass, that in the place where it was said unto them, Ye are not My people, there it shall be said unto them, Ye are the sons of the living God ".[20] The NOT-MY-PEOPLE have nationally, in this Christian dispensation become MY PEOPLE[21] and " sons of [the living] God ".[22]

In the *Venite,* written nearly three thousand years ago and possibly used in the Temple worship, we sing, " O come, let us sing unto the Lord: let us heartily rejoice in the strength of our salvation . . . For He is the Lord our God: and we are the PEOPLE OF HIS PASTURE, and the SHEEP of His hand ". Why have these words been sung *every day* in our National Church since the days of the Apostles unless they are true? Surely it is the greatest presumption to claim to be Christ's sheep if in fact we are not so. Moreover, these verses continue, " Today if ye will hear His voice, harden not your hearts as in the provocation, and as in the day of temptation in the wilderness; when your fathers tempted Me, proved Me, and saw My works ", thus again acknowledging our ancestry.

In the *Te Deum* we sing, " We therefore pray Thee, help THY SERVANTS whom Thou hast REDEEMED with Thy precious blood ". The Bible tells us that Israel is God's SERVANT NATION,[23] that Christ is the REDEEMER of Israel,[24] and that Israel has now become a CHRISTIAN NATION. Peter, writing to *Israelite* Christians, says, " Forasmuch as ye know that ye were not REDEEMED with corruptible things, as silver and gold, from your vain conversation received by tradition from your fathers; but with the precious blood of Christ, as of a lamb without blemish and without spot ".[25] Then we sing, " O Lord, save THY PEOPLE: and bless THINE HERITAGE ", the very same as was prayed by Israel of old.[26]

Also in Morning Prayer we sing another Israel song, the *Benedicite,* which is the song of thanksgiving of Daniel's three companions from the burning fiery furnace. Here again, we sing " O let ISRAEL bless the Lord: praise Him, and magnify Him for ever . . . O ye SERVANTS of the Lord, bless ye the Lord: praise Him, and magnify Him for ever ".

Then notice the *Benedictus* which commences, " Blessed be the Lord God of ISRAEL; for He hath visited and redeemed HIS

THE RUINS OF GLASTONBURY ABBEY

Thy servants think upon her stones: and it pitieth them to see her in the dust" (Psalm 102:14, Prayer Book). Splendid as they are, the ruins give little idea of the magnificence of the Abbey as it formerly existed. The photograph shows the choir of the Great Church of St. Peter and St. Paul, the Eastern piers of the tower, the nave beyond, and, in the distance, St. Joseph's Chapel. A marker in the turf indicates the site of King Arthur's tomb.

THE CHURCH AT PRIDDY

The tiny hamlet in the Mendip Hills retains a tradition of Jesus having been there — "As sure as our Lord was at Priddy".

PEOPLE, and hath raised up a mighty salvation for us in the house of His servant David; as He spake by the mouth of His holy prophets, which have been since the world began: that we should be saved from our enemies, and from the hands of all that hate us; to perform the mercy promised to our forefathers, and to remember His holy covenant to perform the oath which He sware to our forefather Abraham, that He would give us, that we being delivered out of the hands of our enemies might serve Him without fear, in holiness and righteousness before Him, all the days of our life ".[27] Notice this *national* assertion that God's oath to Abraham has been kept.

In the *Jubilate Deo* we sing, " O be joyful in the Lord all ye lands: serve the Lord with gladness, and come before His presence with a song. Be ye sure that the Lord He is God: it is He that hath made us, and not we ourselves; we are HIS PEOPLE, and the SHEEP OF HIS PASTURE ".[28]

Following the Lord's Prayer when we pray " Thy kingdom come, Thy will be done in earth, as it is in heaven ",[29] the priest and people say in turn, " O Lord, shew Thy mercy upon us ", " And grant us Thy salvation ";[30] " O Lord, save the King "; " And mercifully hear us when we call upon Thee "; " Endue Thy ministers with righteousness ", " And make THY CHOSEN PEOPLE joyful ". The priest says, " O Lord, save THY PEOPLE ", and the congregation responds, " And bless THINE INHERITANCE ".

In the order for Evening Prayer we sing the *Magnificat* in which we proclaim, " He remembering His mercy hath holpen His servant Israel: as He promised to *our forefathers*, Abraham and his seed, for ever ".[31]

In the *Cantate Domino* we proclaim that " He hath remembered His mercy and truth toward the HOUSE OF ISRAEL: and all the ends of the world have seen the salvation of our God ".[32]

In the *Nunc Dimittis* we sing that Christ is " a light to lighten the Gentiles, and . . . the glory of THY PEOPLE ISRAEL ", Again we acknowledge that Christ has been the glory of our people, that Britain is a Christian nation.

In the *Deus Misereatur* we sing, " God be merciful unto us, and bless us; and shew us the light of His countenance, and be merciful unto us: that Thy way may be known upon earth, Thy saving health among all nations . . . God shall bless US; and all the ends of the world shall fear Him ". This again shows a recognition of our responsibility as a Christian nation to be a blessing to the whole world.

The *Litany* also acknowledges our Israelite ancestry. We pray, "Remember not, Lord, our offences, nor the offences of our forefathers; neither take Thou vengeance of our sins: spare us, good Lord, spare THY PEOPLE, whom Thou hast redeemed with Thy most precious blood, and be not angry with us for ever". We also make request, "O Lord, arise, help us, and deliver us for Thine honour". Here we acknowledge that the honour of God is involved where the defence of His people is concerned. The Lord swore to deliver His people ISRAEL. If Britain is not Israel then for all these centuries we have been guilty of the grossest presumption in charging God with the responsibility of our defence.

Space precludes our pointing out the very many other features in the Book of Common Prayer which reveal our national identity, but we trust that the reader will study the Book for himself. It has a beauty and clarity of expression unsurpassed in the Englisn language and once the great truth as to the identity and mission of our people is understood, it becomes a source of untold blessing and inspiration.

The Book of Common Prayer is part of our priceless heritage. Its precious truths have been zealously guarded for hundreds of years. We believe it reveals not only God's purpose for the nation but His plan for the whole world. How tragic then that so many today are willing to abandon it in favour of new forms in which these precious truths are lost. And how amazing that there are yet millions who are conversant with the Prayer Book and yet remain in ignorance as to the scriptural identity of our people.

Yet even this is the fulfilment of Scripture. The Bible says, "For the LORD hath poured out upon you the spirit of deep sleep, and hath closed your eyes: the prophets and your rulers, the seers hath He covered. And the vision of all is become unto you as the words of a book that is sealed, which men deliver to one that is learned, saying, Read this, I pray thee: and he saith, I cannot; for it is sealed: and the book is delivered to him that is not learned, saying, Read this, I pray thee: and he saith, I am not learned. Wherefore the Lord said, Forasmuch as this people draw near Me with their mouth, and with their lips do honour Me, but have removed their heart far from Me, and their fear toward Me is taught by the precept of men: therefore, behold, I will proceed to do a marvellous work among this people, even a marvellous work and a wonder: for the wisdom of their wise men shall perish, and the understanding of their prudent men shall be hid ".[33]

Again the Bible says, " Who is blind, but My servant? or deaf, as My messenger that I sent? who is blind as he that is perfect, and blind as the LORD's servant? ".[34] " For I would not, brethren, that ye should be ignorant of this mystery, lest ye should be wise in your own conceits; that blindness in part is happened to Israel, until the fulness of the Gentiles be come in. And so all Israel shall be saved: as it is written, There shall come out of Sion the Deliverer, and shall turn away ungodliness from Jacob: for this is My covenant unto them, when I shall take away their sins ".[35]

The day of Israel's awakening fast approaches!

[1] Ezekiel 18: 27
[2] 1 Timothy 2: 1-2
[3] Ephesians 5: 18-19
[4] Colossians 3: 16
[5] Matthew 6: 7-8
[6] Matthew 6: 9
[7] Luke 11: 1
[8] 1 Thessalonians 5: 17
[9] Ephesians 6: 18
[10] 1 Corinthians 14: 15
[11] Hebrews 10: 23
[12] Jude 3

[13] 2 Peter 1: 21
[14] Isaiah 53: 6
[15] Matthew 15: 24
[16] 1 Peter 2: 25
[17] 1 John 3: 4
[18] Exodus 20: 1-17
[19] John 20: 23
[20] Hosea 1: 9-10
[21] 1 Peter 2: 9-10
[22] 1 John 3: 1
[23] Isaiah 49: 3
[24] Isaiah 43: 1

[25] 1 Peter 1: 18-19
[26] Psalm 28: 9
[27] Luke 1: 68-75
[28] Psalm 100: 1-3
[29] Matthew 6: 10
[30] Psalm 85: 7
[31] Luke 1: 54-55
[32] Psalm 98: 3
[33] Isaiah 29: 10-14
[34] Isaiah 42: 19
[35] Romans 11: 25-27

CHAPTER TWELVE

THE COMING GREAT AWAKENING

IN June, 1969, it was announced that "Land of Hope and Glory" and "Rule Britannia" would no longer be sung at the last night of the B.B.C. Promenade Concerts at the Royal Albert Hall. Apparently they were deemed to be inappropriate by the powers that be. Britain could no longer claim to be a land of hope and glory; Britannia no longer ruled the waves. Even the image of Britannia had been removed from some of the new decimal coinage. Now Britain's young people were to be denied the opportunity even to express their patriotic emotions.

The Monarchy too is under attack. As we go to press, Prince Philip has told the Canadian people that if they do not want the Monarchy, now is the time to get rid of it. Millions have been shocked by the news that Her Majesty the Queen will not this year make her customary Christmas Broadcast. Everywhere and in every way the British way of life is under attack.

The *Birmingham Post* has spoken of "Britain's immoral leadership of the world". Pornographic literature floods the newsstands. Television, cinema and theatre, have become the media for the blatant portrayal of the most revolting perversion and obscenity. The nation is being satiated with violence and sexual depravity.

Northern Ireland is on the brink of civil war. There has been a wave of violence and bloodshed. Streets and houses have been left as smoking ruins in scenes reminiscent of the 'blitz'. A gallant police force has been subjected to violence and intimidation.

The situation is far worse than many would imagine, yet most of our population is so taken up with pleasure and amusement and the quite legitimate concerns of this life, that they have become blind or else indifferent, to the decay, the corruption and the *deliberate* perversion of our people.

The crisis daily grows worse. The Government staves off one economic crisis after another. Each borrowing of further money to repay a previous loan is hailed as a triumph of financial genius. Meanwhile industry is disrupted by wildcat strikes. Taxation soars. The industrious, efficient and hard-working are punitively taxed in order to provide social benefits for the work-shy and the idle.

Even worse, against the wishes of almost the entire populace, scores of thousands of coloured immigrants—numbers greatly in excess of those officially quoted—continue to flood into the country. An infamous Race Relations Act is passed whereby coloured people, against whom the great majority of British people has no ill-feeling whatever, become a privileged class, while those whose forbears have populated these Islands for anything up to three thousand years are reduced to the status of second class citizens.

Yet, less than 30 years ago, young men sacrificed their lives that Britain might be saved. They laid down their lives for the right of free speech, for the sake of freedom, for the preservation of Christian civilisation. Who would have dreamed that the day would come when we should read such items in the national press as the following from the *Birmingham Post*, 18th October, 1969:

"HINDUS SEEK £2,500,000 FOR TEMPLE: A world-wide appeal to raise funds for a £2½m. Hindu temple is to be launched by the Indian community in Birmingham. They are hoping to raise enough cash to build a temple either in the city centre or in countryside within 10 miles of Birmingham . . . Plans for the big fund-raising drive were announced last night as Indians throughout the Midlands began celebrating one of the most important festivals in the Hindu calendar. Hindus were gathering at four centres in Aston, Handsworth, Wolverhampton and Darlaston, to worship their mother-goddess, Durga."

Notice, if you will, that in this land where the gospel has been preached for more than 1,900 years, the great centres of our population, now almost bereft of their native peoples, have become centres of idol worship and paganism. But then notice this item from the *Daily Telegraph*, October 7th, 1969:

"£750,000 MOSQUE IS DESIGN WINNER: Sir Frederick Gibberd, the London architect, has won an international competition with a £3,000 first award for the design of a mosque to be built at the north-west corner of Regent's Park, near terraces designed by Nash . . . Above the main hall is a dome about 75ft. high and, rising from a pool in the forecourt, will be a 150ft. high minaret. The dome will be covered in gold anodised aluminium and the pinnacle of the minaret faced in dove-grey mosaic. Seen from the park, rising above the trees, the minaret and the gold dome will dominate the site . . . The London Central Mosque Trust promoted the competition for a building which will be the centre point of Moslem religious observance."

God help us! When the minarets and domes of pagan temples rise above the tree-tops of our cities, and the city of London, the very heart and centre of Christian civilisation, becomes the focal point of pagan idolatry, it is time our people cried out to God, " Spare Thy people, O LORD, and give not Thine heritage to reproach, that the heathen should rule over them: wherefore should they say among the people, Where is their God ".[1]

Our leaders have shamefully betrayed the nation. Our politicians have legalised sodomy, abortion and easier divorce, have penalised individual initiative and private enterprise, and have weakened the moral fibre of the people through the welfare state. They have abandoned the Empire, rejected our responsibilities, left us virtually without defence. They have destroyed our capacity for greatness, telling us we must become a part of Europe. They have brought into this land hundreds of thousands of coloured immigrants in an attempt to destroy the purity of our racial stock. The Bible says, " O My people, they which lead thee cause thee to err, and destroy the way of thy paths ".[2]

Our church leaders are equally to blame. It is they who have discarded the Word of God, who have taught socialist egalitarianism and an imaginary " equality " of all races. It is the leaders of the churches who have been willing to compromise Bible truth for the sake of a very questionable unity: the *Series II* Communion Service is a case in point. It is they who have encouraged the permissive society. It was an Anglican Bishop's sponsorship of a filthy book that opened the floodgates to a veritable deluge of pornographic literature. No wonder then that crime and violence, decadence and immorality, are on the increase. The Bible says, " The wicked walk on every side, when the vilest men are exalted ".[3]

Again the Bible says, " I have seen also in the prophets of Jerusalem an horrible thing: they COMMIT ADULTERY, and WALK IN LIES: they STRENGTHEN ALSO THE HANDS OF EVILDOERS, that none doth return from his wickedness: they are all of them unto Me as Sodom, and the inhabitants thereof as Gomorrah. Therefore thus saith the LORD of hosts concerning the prophets; Behold, I will feed them with wormwood, and make them drink the water of gall: for from the prophets of Jerusalem is PROFANENESS GONE FORTH INTO ALL THE LAND. Thus saith the LORD of hosts, Hearken not unto the words of the prophets that prophesy unto you: they make you vain: they speak A VISION OF THEIR OWN HEART, and not out of the mouth of the LORD . . . I HAVE NOT SENT THESE PROPHETS, yet they ran: I HAVE NOT SPOKEN TO THEM, yet they prophesied. But if they had stood in My counsel, and had caused My people to hear My words, then they should have *turned them from their evil way, and from the evil* of their doings ".[4]

All our troubles stem from the fact that our people have been kept in ignorance of their place in the purposes of God. The Bible says, " My people are destroyed for LACK OF KNOWLEDGE ".[5] Again the Bible says, " Hear, O heavens, and give ear, O earth: for the LORD hath spoken, I have nourished and brought up children, and they have rebelled against Me. The ox knoweth his owner, and the ass his master's crib: but Israel DOTH NOT KNOW, My people DOTH NOT CONSIDER ".[6]

The only hope for our nation is a return to the Bible, to faith in God, and to *faith in ourselves as a people raised up of God to fulfil a specific purpose in the world.* Sir Arthur Bryant has said, " This off-shore island . . . having lost an empire has still to find a destiny ". The Bible says, " Where there is no vision, the people perish: but he that keepeth the law, happy is he ".[7]

We need as never before to examine our traditions, to rediscover our heritage, to REALISE that we are a people chosen of God to fulfil a special purpose in the world. Party politics *alone* will not save the nation, nor will " soul-saving " evangelism divorced from its context of national salvation. God's plan for our nation, for our Church, for our lives as individuals, is clearly revealed in His Word. The only hope for our nation is a great resurgence of CHRISTIAN NATIONALISM, a belief in the gospel of the Lord Jesus Christ, a conviction of our calling to be a CHRISTIAN NATION. The Bible says, " Blessed is the nation whose God is the LORD; and the people whom He hath chosen for His own inheritance ".[8] " Righteousness exalteth a nation: but sin is a reproach to any people ".[9]

That is the purpose behind this book. The reason for our gathering together the many traditions relating to the coming of the gospel to these Islands is that our people might be awakened to their glorious heritage. After this great length of time it is impossible to know with absolute certainty whether all that we have related is correct in every detail. But of the fact that Britain was the first people *nationally* to embrace the Christian faith, and of the fact that our nation under God has given Christian civilisation to the world, there can be NOT THE SLIGHTEST DOUBT. So great and marvellous has been the fulfilment of the promises of God.

Moreover, we dare to say that our nation yet faces the greatest revival we have ever known. While the very powers of darkness seem about to engulf our nation, yet the Bible promises a coming great awakening when the nation shall recognise the hand of God in its past history, and shall turn to the Lord in faith and penitence and humility. " Then will I sprinkle clean water upon you, and ye shall be clean: from all your filthiness, and from all your idols, will I cleanse you. A NEW HEART also will I give you, and a NEW SPIRIT will I put within you: and I will take away the stony heart out of your flesh, and I will give you an heart of flesh. And I will put My Spirit within you, and cause you to walk in My statutes, and ye shall keep My judgments, and do them. And ye shall dwell in the land that I gave to your fathers; and YE SHALL BE MY PEOPLE, and I WILL BE YOUR GOD . . . Not for your sakes do I this, saith the Lord GOD, be it known unto you: be ashamed and confounded for your own ways, O house of Israel . . . Thus saith the Lord GOD; I WILL YET FOR THIS BE INQUIRED OF BY THE HOUSE OF ISRAEL, TO DO IT FOR THEM ".[10]

Thank God, the tide is beginning to turn. Thousands of people throughout the land are becoming increasingly concerned at the nation's plight. A reaction is setting in against the floodtide of immorality, against the permissive society, against violence on the television screen. Hundreds are awakening to the fact that there is a systematic plot to destroy us. May we not then take hold of the promise of God that, " If My people, which are called by My name, shall *humble* themselves, and *pray*, and *seek my face*, and *turn from their wicked ways;* then will I HEAR from heaven, and will FORGIVE their sin, and will HEAL their land ".[11]

Above all, now at this present time, we need to realise that the moral degeneration which has overtaken our people, together with the attack on patriotism and the British way of life, is part of the most diabolically-inspired plot ever conceived against the British people, and which has as its objective the obliteration of the Western world and the destruction of Christian civilisation. (Write for a FREE copy of *The Plot against the Throne.*) How many realise that high-ranking members of the present Government are humanists and atheists and ENEMIES of Christ?

Today our nation is again at war. We face an enemy far greater, more subtle and more dangerous than any we have faced in all our history. Today we are fighting once again for our very existence, not, as in 1940, a Battle of Britain, but, as never before, a Battle FOR Britain, in which the very future of Christian civilisation is at stake.

We dare not lose this battle. Moreover, we do not believe that the battle shall be lost. We dare to believe that hundreds and thousands and tens of thousands and hundreds of thousands are going to rise up to meet the challenge of this hour. The Bible says, " When the enemy shall come in like a flood, THE SPIRIT OF THE LORD SHALL LIFT UP A STANDARD AGAINST HIM ".[12]

will make of thee a Great Nation GENESIS 12.2

THE ENTIRELY UNCONDITIONAL
NATIONAL BIRTHRIGHT
(GENESIS 12;2, 13;16, 15;5, 17;1-8, 17;16, 18;18, 22;16-18, 24;60,&c.)

The Abrahamic Covenant

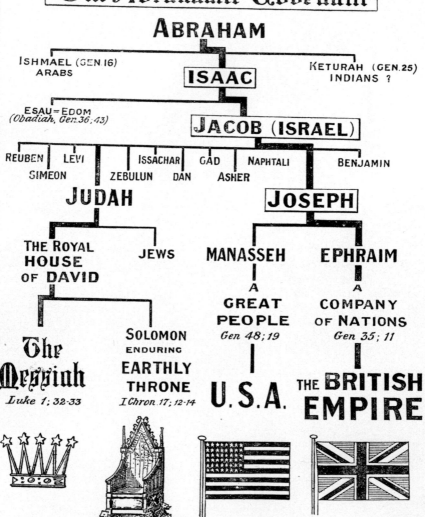

ABRAHAM

ISHMAEL (GEN.16)
ARABS

KETURAH (GEN.25)
INDIANS ?

ISAAC

ESAU=EDOM
(Obadiah, Gen.36;43)

JACOB (ISRAEL)

REUBEN | LEVI | ISSACHAR | GAD | NAPHTALI | BENJAMIN
SIMEON | ZEBULUN | DAN | ASHER

JUDAH

JOSEPH

THE ROYAL
HOUSE
OF DAVID

JEWS

MANASSEH

EPHRAIM

A
GREAT
PEOPLE
Gen 48;19

A
COMPANY
OF NATIONS
Gen 35; 11

The
Messiah
Luke 1; 32-33

SOLOMON
ENDURING
EARTHLY
THRONE
I Chron.17; 12-14

U.S.A.

THE BRITISH
EMPIRE

The qualities which saved Britain in two world wars are again being summoned in this crisis hour. The nation is crying out for inspired leadership, and those whom God will use will be men of strong religious faith. There is no place for the timid, the faint-hearted, the compromisers, the weak-kneed. What is needed are people with faith in God, men of unswerving loyalty and devotion, men of courage, men of conviction, people who will unitedly stand together and resist the common enemy.

The writer is privileged to direct such a movement to which hundreds, yes thousands, of loyal Christian patriots are respond-ing. This work of God stands for patriotism, for loyalty, for sound politics based upon the Word of God, for integrity in public life, for sanctity of home and family, for decency and morality, for the faith once delivered to the saints,[13] for the Christian gospel as it has been stood for in this land for nineteen hundred years, for hard work and industry, for private enterprise, for freedom of speech, for the rebirth of the nation, for GREAT Britain.

This is our vision. This is what God has called us to do. This is the reason for the existence of this work. This is the challenge which God has put before us. Gerald L. K. Smith has said, " *True patriotism is politics surcharged with the dynamic of Christian faith* ".

You may be one whom God has called to share with us in this work. You may be one whom God has raised up to fight the battle with us. What will you do? How will you respond to the challenge? Nearly two thousand years ago, a handful of powerless, cringing, frightened disciples of Christ had barricaded themselves behind locked doors, yet the power of Pentecost transformed their lives so that they went forth to turn the world upside down. The same can happen today as men and women will respond to the challenge of Christ to lift the nation out of the mire of sin and degradation. The battle shall be won, but by men and women with Christian faith, of courage and of vision, and empowered by the Spirit of God, " Not by might, nor by power, but by My Spirit, saith the LORD of hosts ".[14]

Some of you who read these words are committed Christians. God calls you to understand the issues that are at stake, to re-commit your life to Christ. Some of you who read this are con-scious for the first time of the call of God upon your life. The Bible says that you can be *saved*, that you can have the *assurance* of salvation, that you can be *filled with the Holy Spirit* as were God's servants in Bible days. The Bible says, " REPENT, and BE BAPTIZED every one of you in the name of Jesus Christ for the remission of sins, and ye shall receive THE GIFT OF THE HOLY GHOST ".[15]

And now you have read this book. You have seen the challenge. You know that what you have read is the TRUTH of God. You know that you personally are involved, that there is a decision which YOU have to make. May God give you grace to see the crisis for what it is, and to stand with us in this vital work.

[1] Joel 2: 17
[2] Isaiah 3: 12
[3] Psalm 12: 8
[4] Jeremiah 23: 14-16, 21-22
[5] Hosea 4: 6

[6] Isaiah 1: 2-3
[7] Proverbs 29: 18
[8] Psalm 33: 12
[9] Proverbs 14: 34
[10] Ezekiel 36: 25-37

[11] 2 Chronicles 7: 14
[12] Isaiah 59: 19
[13] Jude 3
[14] Zechariah 4: 6
[15] Acts 2: 38

In order to keep this book within a reasonable compass, the contents have been exceedingly condensed. The reader is strongly recommended to re-read the book four or five times, to look up all the Scripture references and examine them in their context, and to write for the other books mentioned in these pages. A *Concordance*, enabling the reader to link together related words and passages from the Bible, will also be of greatest assistance and should be consulted frequently. Every reader of this book is urged to " Study to shew [himself] approved unto God, a workman that needeth not to be ashamed, rightly dividing the Word of Truth."

INDEX